WHAT OTHERS ARE SAYING ABOUT THIS BOOK

"This lively book is a welcome companion to anyone who speaks for a living – or is terrified about giving their first speech."
Jane Applegate, Syndicated columnist & author of "201 Great Ideas for Your Small Business" (Bloomberg Press, 2002)

"Using Barbara's techniques, I find myself much more comfortable and at ease speaking before small and large groups alike. The feedback and invitations I get to come back to speak again are evidence that these techniques are, in fact, very effective in reaching the audience."
Ralph S. Mozilo, Executive Vice President, Countrywide Mortgage Company

"This refreshing and pragmatic book doesn't just focus on technique as others do ... Adjusting your behavioral approach, but never getting to the cause of the stress in speech making. This gets to the cause."
Dawn Green, Vice President, Shafer Advertising

"From CEO's and professional speakers to novice presenters, Barbara's approach is instantly usable. Her tips and feedback have helped me immensely."
Karen Caplan, President, Frieda's, Inc.

"Exciting and useful ... For anyone having a hard time 'getting over themselves'. Formulating a two-hour seminar for our staff, I've used this book as the basis in my preparation."
Sal LaScala, Exec. Vice President, Turner Construction Company

"Barbara's seminars and, now, her book have a 'Zen-like' quality... Enlightening through direct, intuitive insights. Her book spells out the many choices that empower and liberate a presenter ...turning the most terrifying of challenges into a fun opportunity."
David A. Reichel, Ph.D., Director of Compensation, Qualcomm

2nd Edition

GETTING OVER YOURSELF

A Guide to Painless Public Speaking
and More

Barbara Rocha

Bouldin Hill Press
Pasadena 2004

GETTING OVER YOURSELF
A Guide to Painless Public Speaking—and More

By Barbara Rocha

Published by:

 **Bouldin Hill Press**
Post Office Box 60521
Pasadena, CA 91116-6521 U. S. A.

Rocha, Barbara
    Getting over yourself: a guide to painless public speaking.
1. Public speaking. 2. Self-consciousness. 3. Self-improvement

ISBN 0-9660001-1-0 (pbk.)

Library of Congress Catalog Card number 2003114624

Ordering information may be found on page 212

Second Edition
10 9 8 7 6 5 4 3 2 1

TABLE OF CONTENTS

Introduction   1

Section One

Managing Your Mind

Once you change the head, the body's easy.

Chapter 1   How To Get Out of Your Own Way and Become Invisible   7
Chapter 2   Overcoming Nervousness, Keeping Your Poise and Focus   15
Chapter 3   Avoiding the Pitfalls of Perfection   25
Chapter 4   Conquering Fear and Panic   31
Chapter 5   Listen Well and Connect with Your Audience   45
Chapter 6   Dealing with Intimidation   55
Chapter 7   Think Like an Audience   61
Chapter 8   Winning the Mind Game   77
Chapter 9   Coping with a Hostile Audience   89

Section Two

Managing Your Body

Your body communicates more powerfully than your voice

Chapter 10   Controlling Your Feet, Hands and Voice   99
Chapter 11   Letting Go of the Lectern, Notes, and Other Crutches   115

Section Three

Managing Your Words

A well-organized presentationrelaxes you and your audience.

Chapter 12   Coping with Time, Organizing, Using Humor   127
Chapter 13   Creating Effective Visual Aids and Using Them Properly   161

Section Four

Managing Your Success

You just keep getting better.

Chapter 14   How Reluctant Speakers Become Polished Presenters   177

Section Five

Managing Your Life

Now what? These principles can help in every area of your life.

Chapter 15   How Getting Over Yourself Can Help You At the Gym,
              with Your Kids, Asking for Directions, and In Job Interviews 189

Bumper Sticker Philosophy of Speaking   203

Index   205

ABOUT THE AUTHOR

Barbara Rocha, a nationally known speaker, trainer, speech coach, author and consultant, is Director of Barbara Rocha and Associates, a communications training and consulting firm based in Pasadena, California. Over the past 27 years, in addition to speaking and coaching, she has conducted training seminars for well over 10,000 business professionals. These seminars teach verbal and written communications; they are tailored to the specific needs of clients. Her other services include keynote speaker, conference session leader, personalized coaching and speech preparation.

Ms. Rocha earned her B.A. from UCLA and did graduate study at California State University where she earned her M.A. in History, writing a thesis analyzing the speaking ability of Winston Churchill.

Her clients include such companies as Ericsson Turkey, *The San Franciso Chronicle,* Turner Construction, Universal Music Group, Southern California Edison, and Verizon. She also, as an independent contractor, conducts courses for the American Management Association.

For information about consulting, coaching, or workshops, call 1-888-800-2001, visit her website at www.BarbaraRocha.com, or e-mail her at Barbara@BarbaraRocha.com.

Preface

Soon after first edition of this book appeared in print, it became apparent how useful it would be to identify other areas of life where getting over ourselves could produce superior results. We received letters and e-mails telling how they had used the principles to improve golf scores, help their kids with school assignments, do a better job as lay readers in church, and even enhance their social skills.

The conclusion was that if it affects every area of life, we'd better let everyone know about it. Thus, we've added Managing Your Life to this new edition. Because it becomes clear that anything I can do, I can do better, if I just get out of the way.

My deepest thanks to all who so greatly helped me get this message into print with advice, suggestions, ideas, and physical and moral support. My friend and educated reader Kari Helman.

Including my friend Kari Helman's careful reading of the new material, and, once again, Peter Madary for his dedication to the illustrations, my business associate, Jay Bell (without whom there wouldn't be a new edition) and Pam Steffen for a myriad of details.

Author's Notes

My career conducting seminars for improving public speaking stemmed from my own fear of speaking, considering it a potentially terminal activity. Learning the secrets of overcoming the nervous palpitations brought on by the curse of a public presentation compelled me to share the secrets with fellow sufferers.

Our fears start with a list of questions such as: What will they think if I tell a joke and no one laughs? If I lose my place in my notes? If I stumble on the way to the platform? If I leave something out? What if I finish too early or too late? What if they just don't care about what I have to say?

What will they think if I have a slide in the wrong place? If I don't know the answer to a question? If I'm less than perfect? What will they think? (WWTT?)

It was a turning point in my life when I realized what a waste of time that is, because "they" aren't thinking about me at all. I had wasted years imagining that what I was doing mattered to people.

What a relief to discover that it was what *they* were doing that mattered to them. They were really thinking about *themselves*. They were thinking about their own jobs, their families, responsibilities, their comfort and security.

And that's what they're thinking about when they come to hear your presentation. It could be deflating to realize no one's focused on you, but think how free that could make you when you're giving a presentation.

You can be yourself. You can talk like yourself. You can say what you have to say in your audience's terms. You'll be invisible because they'll be focused on your message. Not you!

That's the basis of this book. Getting over yourself is about losing the fears and ineffective delivery that come with being focused on yourself instead of your audience and their needs.

The content is organized into five main sections: Managing Your mind, Managing Your Body, Managing Your Words, Managing Your Success, and Managing Your Life.

It begins with developing the right attitude. What follows will be the poise and comfort that come with knowing you believe in what you're saying. Your techniques and your delivery will continually improve as you expand your empathy and your connection with your audience and as you learn to stay out of your own way.

Everything reminds me of a song, so I sing a lot. My children have told me my singing embarrassed them when they were younger and trying to establish friendships with kids raised by "normal" parents. Anyway, that's why song titles and lyrics pop up throughout the book. If they help make a point more memorable, they've done their job. If they need updating, apply your own.

Songs often speak to universal issues, and I hope the principles of *Getting Over Yourself* might do the same. It's primary function is to help you become a confident and poised speaker; I hope that along the way, you'll find application for these ideas in other areas of your life. (Someone in my first class improved her bowling average 20 points after taking the class.) Getting outside of yourself can yield remarkable benefits in all your interpersonal relationships. Enjoy the journey!

How I learned to stop worrying and love speaking

INTRODUCTION

People would rather die than speak in public. Polls back this up. Yet most of us will face an audience at some point in our lives at work, church or school.

By reading this book, you can *learn* the principles of comfortable, effective public speaking.

You can learn how to get over being nervous.

You might even discover you enjoy public speaking!

So what does this book offer that others on the subject don't? Real-life advice on coping with the sleepless nights and haggard days prior to your big speech or presentation—advice that has helped the thousands of prospective speakers who have attended our three-day seminars overcome their fears and become better communicators.

. . . .

Attitude Adjustment: Get a positive attitude and get rid of the anxiety.

. . . .

"Before I took your course, I was an awful public speaker," said Bob, chairman and CEO of a large company. "I spent hours preparing, worrying and otherwise wasting my time while increasing my stress and anxiety levels before the presentation, followed by endless hours of post-presentation self-flagellation. By focusing on the basic elements you teach, and by practice, I have become a polished presenter."

If you want to learn how to change panic into poise and become a truly fearless public speaker, read on.

The principles in this book are based on my own experiences. Many times before a speech, I would feel my heart racing and my mind reeling. I became determined to overcome those feelings. Once I learned the secrets of pain-free and relaxed public speaking, I felt compelled to share them with everyone.

Here's the premise to my method: Speaking is primarily a mental activity. No amount of technique will disguise an unsound mental and emotional structure. Fix the structure first, then work on the exterior details—an easy thing to do on a solid foundation.

Good public speaking is seven parts attitude and three parts mechanics (organization, body language and rhetorical devices). Most beginning speakers find the mechanics easy to learn. But starting with these elements, rather than with an attitude adjustment, is like slapping fresh paint on a flaky surface—it looks better for a while, but the underlying problem remains.

SALLY FORTH   **BY GREG HOWARD**

Reprinted with special permission of King Features Syndicate

You can wow an audience with a forceful message and a good attitude. You will bore and possibly annoy them if you have a bad attitude, even if your technique is pretty good. Technique alone will not enable you to connect with your audience—and you must connect to communicate. Make no mistake: There is no audience where this is not true.

If you want to communicate, if you want to bring about change, if you want to be effective, focus on connecting, not on data and words. My advice: If you're not going to figure out how to connect with any given audience, don't waste your time trying to decide what to tell them.

How can you assess your attitude?

You have a good attitude if you can answer yes to the following questions:

- Do you expect to do a good job?

- Do you expect to have a good time?

- Do you expect the audience to respect you and respond to your message?

But your attitude needs to change if you answer yes to these questions:

- Do you expect to have problems remembering your material?

- Do you expect to have problems controlling your mind, your tongue or your body?

- Do you expect to be ridiculed by your audience?

. . . .

If you want to communicate, connect with your audience

. . . .

Attitude must be fixed where it begins—inside your head. So let's begin by clearing up some misconceptions, banishing unproductive attitudes and reinforcing some concepts you know instinctively are effective.

SECTION ONE

MANAGING YOUR MIND

ONCE YOU CHANGE THE HEAD, THE BODY'S EASY

BLONDIE   By Dean Young

Reprinted with special permission of King Features Syndicate

1

"Don't Worry, Be Happy"

"This Ain't The Way To Have Fun, Son"

Rose, a successful graphic designer, had to give a talk about puppets when she was in the 9th grade. She was anxious because she didn't have any real interest in puppets and didn't want to get up in front of the class.

On the big day, she packed her puppets in a paper bag and trudged off to school. During her speech, she reached into the bag to pull out her props, but instead of puppets, all she found was a loaf of bread. Devastated, she swore she'd never speak in public again.

Rose "learned" from that experience that speaking in public is humiliating and degrading.

What she *should* have learned was "check your props."

Like Rose, many people are convinced that public speaking is synonymous with pain.

The key to avoiding pain, Rose would learn many years later, is this: Get Over Yourself.

I learned this in 8th grade cooking class. Unfortunately, it took me 20 years to realize what I'd learned. I blame that partly on being in the 8th grade and partly on resistance to an unpopular teacher.

Before class started one day, I asked the teacher what we were going to cook.

"I don't like that," I said of the day's menu.

"Who cares what you like!" the teacher shot back.

I was shocked! But from that experience comes speech lesson No. 1, which you can write in big bold letters on your bathroom mirror: "This Isn't About You."

PEANUTS ® By Charles M. Schulz

PEANUTS reprinted by permission of United Feature Syndicate, Inc.

Well, if it isn't about you, who is that presentation about? Who is that job interview, that performance appraisal about? It isn't about you or me. No, it fits somehow into a bigger picture: helping the audience learn something, helping the interviewer find the right person to fit into that company, helping the appraising manager make the department and the company function more effectively.

The next time you have to speak, say to yourself, "This isn't about me." Then pause. Ask yourself, "If the reason I've been asked to do this isn't just to torment me, what *is* the purpose? What possible reason could there be to give this information to this group?"

For better perspective, put a little distance between yourself and the assignment; look at the big picture. Better perspective will make you a happier speaker.

"I Ain't Got No Body"

Have you ever wished you could phone in your presentation? Wished that all those people weren't staring at you? Longed to be invisible?

Well, getting over yourself makes you invisible.

Here's how it works: When you focus on sharing your message with your audience, instead of focusing on yourself, *they'll* focus on your message, too. When they're focused on your message, they're not thinking about you, and voila! You're practically invisible.

• •

To be invisible: Focus on helping your audience.

• •

Let's say that during your presentation last month, you got one of your transparencies upside-down and you left out a point you wanted to make. You've prepared and practiced for your next presentation, but you can't stop thinking about what happened last month, since you're convinced your audience will be looking for you to slip up again.

If you keep focusing on last month's mishaps, you're really focusing on yourself, instead of on your message. You will look and sound uncertain, and will therefore be highly visible. And you've increased the odds that your audience *will* remember last month, too.

Your freedom stems from this: Realistically, your audience has had other things to think about besides you since your last presentation. Don't force them to remember the past. Give them enough ideas to keep them in the present.

"Now You See Me, Now You Don't"

One woman learned about keeping the audience tuned in to her message the hard way. During a speech in one of our seminars, she lost her train of thought, became totally self-conscious and sat down, instead of finishing.

During a break, she and the instructor analyzed the route her mind had taken when she blanked out and talked about how to keep it from happening again. In her next speech, she dove into her subject with passion and gave absolutely no thought to her earlier failure. Focused on convincing her audience of the rightness of this cause, she was invisible and invincible. No one thought less of her because of her earlier performance; they delighted in her success on *this* one.

Another trap to avoid is trying to top the great presentation you gave last month. You end up botching the current one by not participating in it and drawing attention to yourself rather than to your idea.

Keep your listeners focused on your message, and you can stop wondering if they're thinking bad things about you (because they're not). They will be delighted not to have to worry about whether you'll survive to the end of your presentation, and they'll get more from your subject. You will be invisible and you will be appreciated.

"I Wish I Looked A Little Better"

You know how conspicuous you feel when you have a bad hair day?

Or how great you feel when you've lost some weight?

And how you expect other people to react immediately to even the slightest change in your appearance?

All the things that are *so* conspicuous to us about our appearance go quite unnoticed by others. You get a new hairdo, shave your mustache, grow a mustache, get eyeglasses, switch to contacts, bob your nose, get false eyelashes, cap your teeth, get braces—it's all the same.

Everyone looks at you and says, "You've changed your hair."

They know something is different, but they don't know what. We don't scrutinize other people's appearance the way we do our own. The majority of things that distress us about our appearance go unnoticed by others. And if they do notice? They really don't care. They note it and move on —unless you're focused on it.

People usually see what they expect to see—which is how you looked last time they saw you. It saves them the trouble of paying attention all the time.

My brother shaved his beard and mustache, and I never noticed; he was disappointed. Hey. I'd seen him for years without them. He looked okay to me.

What we look like and what we do aren't as important to others as we might think, even when we're giving a presentation.

"She Wore Blue Velvet"

When you're deciding what to wear for your presentation, remember how little your appearance really matters to others. In choosing your clothing, employ the two principles we've talked about: 1) This isn't about you; and 2) Be invisible.

If you try to impress, intimidate or dazzle your audience with your clothing, you'll make the wrong choice because you're doing it for the wrong reasons.

Dressing appropriately makes you feel good, and it makes your audience feel appreciated.

Vivian Stringer, a basketball coach at Rutgers University, got it right when she said, "When you talk about 'dress for success,' that indicates something special is about to take place. You pay respect to the event by the way you present yourself."

Dressing inappropriately or uncomfortably makes it hard to be invisible.

BERRY'S WORLD   By Jim Berry

I DON'T LIKE TO JUDGE PEOPLE BY THE WAY THEY LOOK, BUT IN YOUR CASE...

Choosing clothes that will help keep the audience focused on your message means dressing very much as they are dressed, with just a bit more attention to detail —a slightly stronger color, a bolder tie, but nothing to distract them, such as run-down heels, too short a skirt, clashing colors, unpolished shoes, radical hair. Your clothes aren't the point of the presentation; don't make them so.

The poet Henry David Thoreau said, "Beware of ventures requiring new clothes." Presentations don't require new clothes; in fact, it's usually a mistake to buy something new to wear.

The emphasis here is on not *needing* new clothes; they could be your downfall: You might forget to remove the price tag, get blisters from the new shoes, or find you can't gesture in that new jacket.

Wear shoes you've worn before and know are comfortable. Wear clothes that won't gap, slip or bind, and that don't have to be hitched. Help eliminate surprises so you don't suddenly feel this presentation is about you.

I will remember-

Memo to me

It isn't about me.

2

"I Will Survive"

"Everybody Plays The Fool, Sometime"

Here's a piece of good news: You're not the only person who doesn't enjoy speaking in public. As a matter of fact, there are probably people in your company more anxious than you about speaking, and several in your department who are equally uncomfortable. But, just like you, they hide it.

Privately, many people contemplate loosing a primal scream, faking a coma or perhaps developing a rare tropical disease when faced with a speaking assignment.

Knowing upper management's probable reaction to this, and sensing a certain discomfort on the part of peers, few people actually unleash these emotions publicly. So, because you've never seen your co-workers acting the way you feel, you assume they don't mind speaking.

Remember those studies that show the fear of public speaking rating higher than the fear of poverty, death or total incapacity? Are people really more afraid of public speaking than of dying? Well, Howard, a student in one of our early classes, maintained that enemy fire in Vietnam scared him less than speaking in public.

But is being nervous about speaking all that bad? What about all those people who say you have to be nervous to be a good speaker? That without the nervousness, you'd be boring? It's simple: They're wrong. Should you be alive? Yes. Alert? Yes. Interested? Yes. But nervous? No.

BALLARD STREET   By Jerry Van Amerogen

By permission of Creators Syndicate

Think about it. Aren't there activities you look forward to, that you find exciting, pleasant, enjoyable, that don't throw you into a panic? Does the thought of going water-skiing, to the theater, rollerblading, sailing or bird watching give you a spurt of adrenalin? Adrenalin and nervousness are not synonymous. So here's another reason for changing your head: Positive feelings about speaking stop nervousness and contribute energy.

"Just Direct Your Feet To The Sunny Side Of The Street"

You can make your next presentation about four times less stressful by playing a little game with yourself. I'm not usually into tricks, but this one is silly enough to be worth trying, and it really can help: When you're asked to make a presentation, say, "I'll be glad to."

Nip the fear in the bud. If you let panic or discomfort in the door, they'll take over the party. So even if you're saying "I'll be glad to" through clenched teeth, it will make your presentation easier from start to finish.

You can practice this the next time someone asks you to help with a volunteer project. Instead of drooping and droning, "Well, if you can't find anyone else, call me back," try the "I'll be glad to" approach. If you're going to say yes, do it good-naturedly. The amazing thing is that the assignment is much easier and doesn't feel like a chore. Moaning always makes it twice as unpleasant.

"Don't Let The Sound Of Your Own Wheels Drive You Crazy"

I've been nervous and I've been not nervous, and I can tell you this: Not nervous is better. I used to be darned uncomfortable whenever I was in front of an audience. I could be uncomfortable in front of three or four people if I felt they were expecting more of me than I thought I could deliver.

So what's the secret? How do you get over feeling inadequate? Let's look at a typical scenario.

You're ready to go on. Your heart is pounding, your mouth is dry, your knees are weak; you wish it was over. Suddenly, everything you've ever imagined might go wrong flashes before your eyes—that upside-down slide, that tricky word you kept tripping over during practice, the missing budget numbers.

"What if I drop the slides again?"

"What if I forget how many units we shipped last quarter?"

SALLY FORTH By Greg Howard and Craig MacIntosh

Reprinted with special permission of King Features Syndicate

"What if they notice my hands shaking?"

STOP! You're losing control because you've stopped being rational. At this moment it's hard to believe you can take charge, but you can. You can stop the pounding and the terrifying symptoms.

Pause and breathe. Realize: "This isn't about me. This isn't about showcasing me. This is about telling them what happened last quarter so they can confirm our recent decisions (or recognize that we need to alter our course)."

Keep breathing: Focus on why you're there and stop the mental stampede.

HAGAR THE HORRIBLE   By Dik Browne

Reprinted with special permission of King Features Syndicate

Knowing that you're in control of your focus—and therefore in control of what you're thinking—builds confidence. You can think rationally while standing in front of a group. It's a big key to getting over yourself.

"When you come to a crossroads take it." —Yogi Berra

Controlling your focus means you get to choose what's going on in your head. That crossroad is the decision to be comfortable or uncomfortable when you give a presentation.

Making the right choice gives you a great feeling of power.

And you *can* choose to feel good about speaking.

This is a book about choices, and to put it plainly, nervousness is a choice. It's often an unconscious choice (a choice by default), but a choice nonetheless.

It's like the default position on your computer. When you turn on your computer, the default font is in place; the default margins are in place. If you don't change the default, that's what you'll have.

If nervousness is your default position before you speak, take heart. You can change that, too. Here's how: Instead of worrying about yourself and your chances of succeeding, think about 1.) Why the listeners need the information, and 2.) How you can help them by giving it to them.

For instance, let's say a team from your company is making a presentation to an important client in hopes of winning a big contract.

You could choose to focus on your fear of missing your cue; worry that you won't explain things clearly enough; and obsess about leaving out vital information, all of which will make you nervous and keep you from confidently presenting your information.

Or you could focus on why this audience needs the information. For instance: The client needs to make an intelligent decision that will make the buyer look good and make the shareholders, the employees, and the boss happy. Focus on showing them how using your services will make their lives easier, how happy other companies have been, and how easy your people are to work with.

You have a choice. Think about yourself and everything that can go wrong. Or think about sharing information and helping the audience. The right choice makes you invisible and highlights what your company has to offer. The wrong choice encourages them to nit-pick.

One fuels fear. The other makes you comfortable.

"Have You Ever Had To Make Up Your Mind?"

Of course you have, (and it's not often easy and it's not often kind). But in this case, the easy part is that you know the result you're after: to eliminate pain. You know you're going to have to speak if you want to move up the ladder, and you know you don't want to suffer.

Make up your mind to enjoy the presentation. Make up your mind to think about all the ways this information can be useful to particular people or groups in your audience. Make up your mind to stay focused.

It's not about you.

Install a choke chain on your mind, and give it a yank when you feel yourself wandering.

"Oh, no. I gave the wrong number."

Yank!

Correct the number if you need to (without apologizing), and go on.

"Oh no. John just said what I was supposed to say."

Yank!

Regroup. "As John mentioned . . . "

"Oh no. I stumbled on the cord."

Yank! Pause. Refocus. Grin.

"That's why they have me doing presentations, instead of a high-wire act over Niagara Falls."

You have to make up your mind to focus on your message, not yourself.

"What You See Is What You Get" — Flip Wilson

I used to have to ride my bike between two posts spaced about 20 inches apart to get onto the bike path. It was a struggle every time as I tried to squeeze through that space without hitting one of the posts. Until I realized I was looking at the posts trying not to hit them, instead of at the space where I wanted to go. It's the same with speaking—you have to look where you want to go, not at where you don't.

Focus on helping the audience. Realize there are some benefits in the ideas you're expressing. There's gold in them thar thoughts, or at least there's value in them. You must appreciate their value if your audience is going to see them as worthwhile.

Look at it this way: What are the chances of giving a good presentation if you think the material is garbage? What are the chances of giving one if you think you're hopeless? What are the chances if you think the audience is too stupid to understand or appreciate what you're saying?

Guard your thinking. Control what you're "seeing." Garbage in, garbage out. Value yourself, your message and your audience if you want to connect. Because what you see is what you get.

"Keep Your Sunny Side Up"

When my brother, Dave, was in high school, my mother persuaded him (using "Mom Methods") to go to a church-sponsored party he didn't want to go to.

When he got home, she asked him if he'd had a good time. "Of course I had a good time," he retorted. "If I'm going to go, I'm going to have a good time."

. . . .

If you have to give a presentation, have a good time.

. . . .

Chalk one up for big brother. If I'd been the one who had to go, I'd have made sure she knew how miserable she'd made me.

Why suffer? If you have to give a presentation, choose to have a good time.

A petite businesswoman, serving as the luncheon speaker at a large Rotary Club meeting, brought her briefcase with her to the lectern, placed it on the floor and stood on it making her tall enough to reach the microphone. She got a big laugh and bonded with her male audience, making a positive out of the potential negative of being a petite woman in business.

I will remember—

Memo to me

Nervousness is a choice. I can think about myself OR I can think about helping the audience

3

"All You Need Is Love"

"Will You Still Love Me Tomorrow?"

The biggest stumbling block for most of us is wanting to be perfect. Even people who aren't perfectionists feel the pressure to do everything exactly right when they're giving a presentation. We all need to feel loved and approved of.

In giving a presentation, that translates into "If I'm great, they'll appreciate me, think I'm worthy, like me better."

Au contraire. People are more likely to be put off by perfection. If you know people who are perfect and you like them, it's probably in spite of their being perfect, not because of it.

I read recently that we like to see our heroes stumble because it makes us feel better about our own failures. If that's true, why try to become anyone's hero by being perfect?

A better goal might be to focus on helping the audience, on remaining invisible and rolling with the punches. Then if something goes wrong and you don't buckle, the audience will feel better about themselves —they like to think they might do as well under difficult circumstances.

Think of a speaker you've heard who was technically good, but boring. Did you have a hard time identifying with him or the subject? Focusing on being good interferes with connecting with your audience because you're focused on yourself, not on sharing information.

If you're committed to making an effective presentation (instead of a perfect one), consider this: An effective presentation is one the audience leaves knowing what they need to know and considering doing what you want them to do. It's not one in which the speaker does everything perfectly.

"I'm Too Sexy for My Shirt"

Imagine you're giving a presentation to the city council, trying to persuade it to increase funding for homeless shelters.

Everyone in town is there for your full-scale presentation in the civic auditorium—your neighbors, boss, church members, bowling buddies. And you *know* you don't want to embarrass yourself in front of all these people.

The question is, what is most important to you: solving the homeless problem or giving a perfect presentation?

Given only two choices, I'd rather forget some of my facts, drop my notes, get a slide upside-down and have them allocate the money to solve the problem than to get everything right and not get the money.

Perfect posture, gestures, organization and visual aids won't make up for an aura of detachment. On the other hand, connecting with your audience will usually make them empathetic and forgiving. They may even like you if they see you're human.

Don't try to be perfect. It's an unrealistic and self-defeating goal. If your goal is to be perfect, your chances of success are slim and none.

If your goal is to be sure your audience gets the information, you might actually make a perfect presentation. But even if you don't, you're a winner because they'll leave satisfied. And they'll either forget anything that went wrong or admire the way you handled it.

Of course, you need to respect your audience and the occasion: Organize your thoughts before you arrive, dress appropriately, plan your comments and your visual aids with your audience in mind. Practice at least once. That's not the same as aiming for a perfect presentation.

John F. Kennedy paid attention to all the image and all the dress-for-success rules before appearing in public. But once he got there, he turned his whole attention to communicating with the audience.

Richard Nixon, in those famous presidential debates with Kennedy, ignored the image details and focused on the facts, more interested in perfection than in connecting with the audience. Radio listeners gave Nixon the winning edge. TV viewers scored Kennedy as the winner.

Your focus needs to be outward, not inward.

"Que Sera, Sera"

One man I know was called in at the last minute as a substitute to speak before several hundred people. He laid his notes on the lectern, walked away from it to address the crowd and, when he couldn't remember what came next, walked back over to check his next point. He wasn't the least bit apologetic, and the audience wasn't the least bit critical or concerned.

Another speaker, arriving 10 minutes late because of flight and traffic delays, apologized amiably for being late, mentioning the reason, and asked the audience to give him time to be sure his microphone was working properly. He then proceeded to go through the entire test sequence with no sense of pressure. He knew what he had to say was important, and he wasn't going to devalue the message or his audience by rushing the means by which they could hear it.

Another time I saw a grandmotherly woman speak to a builders' convention about the importance of choosing the right color schemes for their model homes. Many in this mostly male audience got up and left the hall before she began, based solely on their perception of her subject and her appearance. She moved the remaining group from cooly polite attention (based on their stereotypical expectations) to full attention. She was genuinely interested in and believed in her subject. Proof of her success: During a break, the audience continued to discuss her topic and how it would affect their projects.

Rather than be perfect, be human.

I will remember -

Memo to me

Most audiences are human. So, I will be human (not perfect) — in my attitude and in my choice of words

4

"Amazing Grace"

"I'm All Shook Up"

Being human presents a problem for most of us. What if we're human and everyone snickers? We're way too concerned about how this presentation might affect our job or our relationships with people in the audience.

It's a case of worrying about "What Will They Think?"—about your clothes, words, visuals and gestures.

Our biggest "What Will They Think" centers on something GOING WRONG. Of course, worrying that something will go wrong will haunt you, practically guaranteeing something will.

Even if you're happily sailing along, something may not go according to plan. The thing to remember is that it's how you handle it, not what went wrong, that has the impact on your audience.

We've all witnessed other people's embarrassing moments. Not everyone handles them the same. Maybe you had friends in high school who made you chuckle when they did something embarrassing. Sometimes everyone chuckles and there's no harm done. And sometimes, everyone is painfully uncomfortable; you've probably seen this happen, too. Unfortunately, it may have been during someone's presentation.

The key is how we respond. If the speaker acts like it's no big deal, we're okay. If she self-destructs, we suffer.

Some people who are good actors pretend they're okay. You might want to try that, but usually you're still churning inside. So if your acting skills aren't what they might be and you'd really rather *stop* the inner turmoil, let's look at another way to deal with it.

"I Guess You Say, What Could Make Me Feel This Way?"

As John Lennon put it, "Life is what happens to you while you're making other plans."

Your audience knows from experience that "stuff happens."

Has "stuff" ever happened to you during a presentation? What was your first thought? Did you feel humiliated? Were you convinced that you confirmed everyone's suspicions—that you're not qualified for your job? How can you continue? You want to say something, but you're absorbed by THE DISASTER.

When something goes wrong anywhere (not just in a speech), we're mortified. We berate ourselves. We take it as a personal imperfection. That's a pretty common approach in life; it's almost the universal approach when you're in front of an audience.

During the regular fund-raising drive for a local PBS station, one of the on-camera volunteers mistakenly held up a giant credit card upside-down. When she became aware of it, she apologized with a giggle, as though she had done something quite wrong, and she kept referring to it apologetically throughout that break.

Later, at the next break, she mentioned it again. And again. It was a minor mistake, easily corrected. It was no big deal—until she made it one. She agonized over it so much, she couldn't let it go. Consequently, neither could we—and we *wanted* to.

"I'll Never Smile Again"

What's the worst thing that could happen?

Prepare yourself. It might actually happen.

The question isn't so much "What can happen?" as "What are you going to do if it does happen?"

Of course, once it happens and you live, you become quite relaxed.

Pat put the slide on upside-down during her presentation in one of our classes, made a second stab at it and got it wrong again. She giggled and kept going, but she never stopped thinking about her mistake. So the final minute of her speech had no punch, and she felt like a miserable failure. In truth, her closing wasn't terrible (as she could see on the videotape), but it wasn't as strong as the rest of the presentation, and she wasn't happy.

In such a situation, it would be appropriate to make a note to work with the equipment and do a run-through before your next presentation. Just make a note. Don't waste time trashing yourself.

During the presentation, there's no point in thinking about crawling into a hole or about what you should have done. Realizing "stuff happens," Pat would have felt better if she had grinned and shrugged it off. Sure, she could have said something, and probably would have made an appropriate remark ("Be glad I didn't show you all four directions") if she hadn't taken it personally. And that's the most important part—not taking it personally.

The worst thing about the experience was her feeling of having failed when it was over. She let a perfectly good presentation be ruined (in her own eyes) by the kind of mistake we all wish wouldn't happen, but which sometimes does.

Lots of times, speaking can feel like tightrope walking—one false step and you're finished. The key to walking a tightrope is keeping your balance; it's also

the key to speaking. If you falter, just pause, regroup and regain your poise (your mental balance).

To keep your mental balance, stop thinking about yourself.

Ask yourself, "How can I make the audience comfortable? How can I put them at ease?"

If you suffer, the audience suffers. It's that simple.

"And Then I Go And Spoil It All By Saying Something Stupid"

I was elated when it dawned on me that when I said or did something stupid, it was because I had lost my focus, or never had it. It's not lack of intelligence that causes this stuff.

What a relief!

We lose our focus all the time, in everyday situations, not just when making presentations. Think about it. The next time you say or do something that makes you wince, check to see if it was lack of focus, like forgetting whom you've phoned by the time they answer. Often we find ourselves thinking of more than one thing at a time, our thoughts darting from one subject to another. We get away with this split focus most of the time. But in front of an audience, it's not only not good for communicating, blanking out is painful.

Recognize mistakes for what they are—lack of focus. And if the occasion is important enough to you, you've got the answer. Pause and refocus.

"Rescue Me"

The easiest (and most painful) thing to do in a crisis is to panic and fast-forward to the death of your career.

You've got to get a grip!

First of all, they're not thinking what you think they're thinking. They feel embarrassed for you. There's not a person in the audience who hasn't worried about what stupid thing he or she might do at some crucial moment, not necessarily limited to speaking engagements.

And there's not a person in the room who hasn't at least once made a world-class blunder in his or her own eyes.

Sure, you think some of those people are too smooth ever to have done anything awkward. But I dare you to imagine anyone getting through elementary school or adolescence without feeling mortified.

When you flounder, they identify with your predicament. They re-live the same gut-wrenching agony they've felt in their own embarrassing moments. They hope you're going to be all right so they can relax. They'd like to help you . . . but that could put them in an embarrassing position.

So it's up to you to let them off the hook. Let them know you're all right.

Dave was feeling tense in front of a large audience. He'd been tripping over words and feeling quite awkward. While he was presenting a scholarship award that involved speech training, he remarked that he could use some of that right about then. The audience laughed, and he felt them (and himself) relax. He was fine. And so were they.

"You May Be Right. I May Be Crazy"

Poise is keeping your wits about you. Poise, you may remember, is mental balance—it means your brain continues to function.

What do you do when the backup bulb in the overhead projector burns out? What do you do when your boss in the audience preempts your remarks while you're on the podium? What do you do when the computer blows up?

At age 12, violinist Midori stopped mid-phrase when one of her strings broke during a concert. She calmly exchanged instruments with the first violinist and continued to play. She behaved so naturally and comfortably, there wasn't time or reason for the audience to become uncomfortable.

Minutes later, another string broke. Again with no fluster, she traded violins with the first violinist and picked up the melody.

When something unexpected happens, you might feel inadequate. You are temporarily unbalanced. Then to cover up, you start babbling—well, maybe not that bad, but it feels like babbling to you, and it doesn't sound all that meaningful to the audience.

Merle by Peter Madary

I WAS SO EMBARRASSED. IT WAS ONE OF THOSE AWKWARD MOMENTS WHEN THERE'S NOTHING TO SAY. SO, OF COURSE, I JUST KEPT ON TALKING!

When you're under control, the audience stays relaxed, confident of your ability to protect them. In order to "get a grip," you need to get control of your thinking so you can get back on track.

How do you do that?

You pause. And breathe.

Don't *do* anything except refocus on your subject and what you're there for.

Pausing and refocusing works because you give your heart and your mind recovery space to catch up and catch on. It seems unnatural to stop talking in front of an audience in the middle of a presentation. Maybe even bizarre. But you've had to learn other things in life that went against your instincts, such as resisting the urge to slam on the brakes when your car skids.

So pause, refocus, and think quietly about what you just said. You can remember what you said and where you're going if you're quiet. It's not the remembering that's hard, it's the being quiet.

Let the audience take care of itself for a minute. You're no good to them until you can take care of yourself.

The speaker's face tells the whole story. In one of our classes, Marlin lost his next point. He immediately refocused to find out where he was and what he wanted to say. No time wasted thinking about himself or his predicament. So he looked focused and in control causing no panic in his audience.

If the flight attendant on your plane panics, you probably do too. But if the attendant continues serving dinner despite that strange noise, you relax. Help your audience relax. Let them know everything is under control.

You can keep everything under control by thinking of the audience members as friends who want you to recover. You'll feel less concerned about the silence, and you'll recall your point more quickly.

"It Had To Be Me, Wonderful Me"

Thinking of your audience as friendly and supportive makes it a lot easier to enjoy what you're doing. Worrying about when you're going to get the hook causes brain lock.

For most presentations, it's pretty clear that it's not about you; if you had to be out of town, someone else would have to make the presentation. The audience needs to be informed or entertained, and if you don't do it, someone else will.

So get over yourself. Talk to these people. They're stuck in their seats by duty or good manners, and you'll either be Batman or the Joker. Stop thinking about what can happen to you, and remember the reason you're speaking to them. There's a benefit to this audience in hearing this information.

Become invisible by remembering: It has to be them, wonderful them.

"Fear Makes You Hurry, Poise Lets You Pause" — Jessica Somers Driver

Fear of being out of control, fear of looking foolish, fear of losing credibility—whatever the fear, it feeds on itself and creates a problem where no real problem existed.

Fear accelerates your heart rate, jams your mind and bullies you into talking before you're ready. It convinces you that silence can kill, that silence will make your audience turn on you.

Poise allows rational thinking. A person who has it is not afraid to be quiet and think.

Look around for examples of poise: people going about their business undisturbed by what other people are thinking, focused only on what they themselves need to accomplish.

An Olympic high-diver stands quietly on the end of the board taking all the time needed to visualize the dive and prepare. She doesn't rush and isn't worried that the crowd will think she's not prepared, or doesn't know how to do the dive.

When you're doing something you're good at (athletics, music, conversation, hobbies), notice that you're not afraid of silence or periods that look to someone watching you as though you're not doing anything. We need quiet times when all the activity is on the inside before we're ready to translate ideas into action. When you watch people going through that process, you respect what they're doing. It's obvious something is going to happen and this draws you in. It's the same in public speaking.

So why do we start talking before we're ready? Because "fear makes you hurry. Poise lets you pause."

Don't start speaking until your brain is in gear.

"You Left Me Just When I Needed You Most"

Starting to speak before you're mentally tuned in may result in brain lock. You find yourself with no idea of who you are or why you're standing there.

For many of us, blanking out in front of an audience qualifies as the worst thing that can happen during a presentation. If it's ever happened to you, you can still recall the anguish. It's this specter that makes us do almost anything to get out of giving a presentation.

Now what?

It's time to analyze just what happens when you blank out. Understanding what causes it will help you get over the past and avoid having it happen again.

Essentially, you lost your focus. You were moving right along, involved with what you were saying, when something broke your concentration.

Try to remember what caused it. Did your boss walk into the room? Were you trying to think ahead to what you were going to say next? Had you just mispronounced a word, given the wrong statistic, stumbled on the projector cord? Whatever happened, you began to worry about yourself and lost your focus.

You're there for a reason; so stop, gather your thoughts, and remember it. The audience needs the information, and the only way you can give it to them is to get back on track.

"Silence Is Golden"

Forgetting terrifies us partly because we're certain that silence is a disgrace. We think of silence as a sign above our heads flashing "LOSER."

Here's some news. That pause which seemed interminable to you probably wasn't even noticed by the audience. Hardly any time passed. But you're sure you've been standing there, tongue-tied, FOREVER.

Pauses are relative.

Albert Einstein explained the theory of relativity this way: "When you sit with a nice girl for two hours, you think it's only a minute. But when you sit on a hot stove for a minute, you think it's two hours. That's relativity."

When you feel uncomfortable during a pause, it's the hot stove part at play.

But wait a minute. Professionals pause all the time and we think they're great. Notice how other people's pauses affect you. Most of the time, you're probably grateful because a pause gives you time to catch up and maybe even to chew on a thought. Pros who pause usually seem quite in control. You go away thinking, "What a great speaker!"

Don't be afraid of silence. Silence can be powerful. Use it to get back on track. Use it to give the audience time to catch up. Use it to participate in what you're saying.

Yes, participate.

That's what you do in an interesting conversation, whether you or someone else is talking. Well, a presen-

PEANUTS® By Charles M. Schulz

PEANUTS reprinted by permission of UnitedFeature Syndicate, Inc.

tation *is* a conversation. But since you've organized your talk around the audience's needs and concerns, you've essentially anticipated their side of the conversation and are now giving your side, as well as responding to theirs. Participate in the conversation. Be there. Take advantage of the power of silence. And remember the wise man who observed, "I'd rather keep my mouth shut and be thought a fool, than to open it and remove all doubt."

"Time Is On My Side"

Pauses are your friends. And they're good for your audience, too.

Then General Colin Powell, addressing Howard University's 1994 commencement, used pauses effectively and offered a great example of participating in a speech and making it feel like a conversation. At one point, he paused appropriately at the end of an idea. As he continued pausing, he quietly looked at a part of the crowd over to the side. He just stood quietly. Looking. It soon became clear there was a disturbance in the audience. He didn't go on speaking. He simply watched. Eventually, he nonchalantly said, "I think it's under control whatever it is." (Pause.) "I think we're okay." (Pause.) "Let me know if you need me up there." (Said with a friendly voice and a smile.)

He showed himself to be in control, and the audience felt undisturbed.

"Fools Rush In"

There's a certain kind of silence that *will* make an audience uncomfortable. That's when the speaker blanks out and panics.

This silence roars through the room, capturing everyone's attention as the speaker shuffles notes, snatches at a glass of water, glances nervously from one unfocused place to the next.

And it is in this condition that the speaker is most likely to blurt out something that was not in the plan.

This kind of silence is nobody's friend. The speaker is miserable, and so is the audience.

This is not a pause. This is self-destruction.

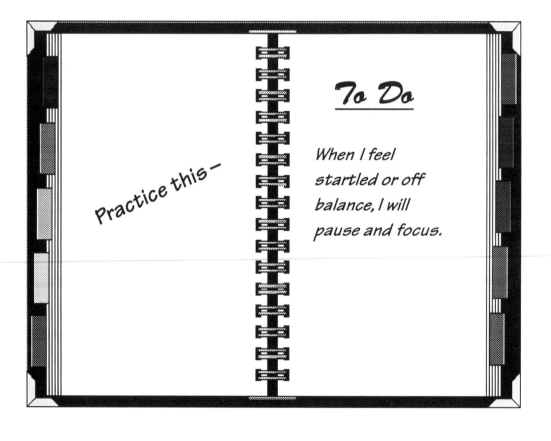

Practice this—

To Do

When I feel startled or off balance, I will pause and focus.

5

"Listen My Children And You Shall Hear"

"Do You Hear What I Hear?"

Have you ever put your foot in your mouth, choked when asked a question, blanked out during a presentation, failed to respond appropriately to an employee with a problem or been stumped as to how to organize your presentation?

There's a one-size-fits-all solution to all of those situations, and it's called listening: Getting tuned into the big picture, rather than your part in the picture. We're not the big picture, we're just one small part of it. Operating from that perspective, it's possible to listen for the right thing to say or do.

Your mother got annoyed with you because you didn't listen. Your teachers harped on you to listen. And now corporate America has taken up the cry. Maybe there's something to it. The fact is, your poise, your mental dexterity, your ability to communicate effectively with one person or a group, depends on your ability to listen, to be aware of the big picture.

"Slip-Sliding Away"

Let's say you're giving a talk. Something in the room distracts you, and you lose your train of thought. You have no idea what you were saying. Now, if that something has distracted the entire audience, it's easy to get back on course because you didn't take it personally and because you're familiar with what you want to say. But if you were the only one distracted, that means you weren't focused on your topic, but yourself. You lost sight of the big picture.

MISTER BOFFO   By Joe Martin

Working from your own agenda blocks proper listening. To listen, focus on solving problems, on increasing productivity, on putting the new policy into effect smoothly. Focus on what's right, not who's right.

Getting yourself out of the way (getting perspective) opens us up to seeing the big picture, making all the ideas in the universe available to you when you need them.

It illustrates Henry Ford's statement, "The air is full of ideas. They're knocking on your head trying to get in. All you have to do is know what you want, forget about it and go about your business."

You know how well your mind works when you're looking at the big picture? You know those times, maybe when someone else is responsible for answering the question or solving the problem. Isn't that when the answer is absolutely clear to you? When you're not feeling any pressure and you're not taking it personally?

That's listening. The ideas are knocking on your head, and you can hear them because you're not cluttered up with who's going to get the credit or the blame, or how you're going to look.

Have you ever gotten home and let go of a problem you'd been wrestling with at work? And has the answer come to you out of the blue, maybe while you were fixing dinner or taking a shower? You've unconsciously stopped trying and started listening. You've let go of worrying about a solution and allowed your mind to "hear" one.

When you blank out in front of an audience you can't "forget about it and go about your business." But it's the attitude that the ideas are knocking on your head trying to get in that will work. If you listen.

Tune in to the big picture, rather than to yourself.

"I Hear Ringing And There's No One There"

Don't you hate that semi-vacant stare accompanied by ill-timed nods that indicate your "listener" would rather be flossing his teeth than talking to you? And don't you hate it when your boss doesn't listen to your ideas for improving company morale? And when your

By permission of Doug Marlette and Creators Syndicate

employees don't hear your reasons for needing diversity training?

Here are three things you can do to combat this:

- Be sure you're paying attention to and interested in what you're saying.

- Notice whether your listeners are paying attention and be aware of what they are paying attention to.

- Don't do it to other people—zone out, that is. Listen to yourself when you're talking, and listen to others when they talk.

This, too, involves getting tuned in to what's going on outside, rather than on yourself. You'll be a better problem solver, and more promotable.

It's that kind of unselfconscious listening that gives you the answers to tough questions, that gets you back on track when you've blanked out, that tells you how to approach this subject with this audience.

People want to be heard. In company after company, people complain they can't get upper management to listen to them. "They don't tell us what's going on. They expect us to buy into these changes, but *they're* not."

Harry Rodenburger (a delegate from Blaine, Washington, to a National Issues convention in Austin, Texas in January 1996) echoed how most of us feel: "We felt refreshed because someone was out there listening to us and cared that we had an opinion."

When your employee (or someone at home) wants to discuss a problem, and you've got a project on your mind, what kind of listening do you do? Do you listen half-heartedly while you continue to massage your own project? Or do you tune in at least long enough to find out how urgent their need is? And if it's the former, how much progress did you make on your own project, and how much progress did you make with their problem?

Paying attention to what you're saying and to what others are saying (being "in the moment") is a multipurpose weapon: It creates allies, keeps you from blanking out, gives you answers you didn't know you knew, makes you a better manager and a more dynamic speaker. All that, just from listening, being tuned in to the big picture, rather than your own agenda.

You Snooze, You Lose

Desperate silences come from lapses in concentration. Go "out to lunch" for a moment, and you'll be gasping for air, simulating a landlocked tuna.

CALVIN AND HOBBES   By Bill Watterson

Someone once asked pianist Vladimir Horowitz what was the most important thing his father-in-law, Arturo Toscanini, ever did. His answer: "Whatever he was doing at the moment, whether it was conducting a symphony or peeling an orange."

Your presentation is what you're doing at the moment. If you want it to be good, it needs to be more important than any client calls you have to make, any random thoughts about what this client might be thinking, or concerns about how little you practiced. Even momentary digressions about whether to include a piece of information that just now occurred to you, or whether or not to correct the number you just gave, can send you down the wrong road.

There's no room here for idle minds. Stay focused. And if something distracts you, pause, refocus, and get on with the job.

You Snore, You Lose More

If you follow a distraction to its natural conclusion, you will lose your mental balance, your train of thought and control.

My high school's motto was "Rowing, not drifting" —a motto to inspire the hearts and minds of any high-school student! Well, even if it didn't work that well on high-school students, it's a good motto for speakers.

Make up your mind. No drifting. Focus on helping the audience. Get over yourself.

If you drift, you lose your audience. You lose their respect. You lose the chance to make a point, change the company, improve profits and productivity. How much more do you want to lose?

"Uptight, Outta Sight"

Think of yourself as the host or hostess. It's your job to make these people comfortable, to set them at ease just as you would at home with your guests. As soon as you get away from how *you're* feeling, your mind will start to work again, and you'll know what to say or do. Make it easy for them to listen to and accept what you're telling them. Reassure them everything's okay so you can move along.

If a guest in your home does something embarrassing, you know just how to reassure him. And if you burn the pudding, you also need to focus on making your guests comfortable, not on your mistake.

If everyone in your audience can see what's gone wrong, mention it so they won't wonder how you could not notice such a thing. If you don't say something about tripping over the cord and landing on the floor, they'll wonder if you're really all right and not hear anything you say. Let everyone know that you're okay, and get on with it. Make them comfortable.

The down side to handling it badly: You make them feel bad about themselves. On the one hand, they sympathize with you and your discomfort. On the other, they may squirm because you're reminding them of their flaws.

You really will know what to say and do if you regain your mental balance and focus on what's going on.

"Walk Right In, Sit Right Down, Daddy Let Your Mind Roll On"

Considering everyone in your audience an equal is good for you and good for your audience. Look at speaking as an opportunity for peers to share ideas.

Even if they have impressive titles (CEO, executive vice president), and regardless of what rung of the corporate ladder they're on, everyone will benefit if you consider them all peers. Your brain will function better; you'll be more confident and more convincing.

It's good for everyone if you're not embarrassed. Let them know everything's all right, and grin, so you can get back to your topic. They can relax and focus on the information instead of worrying about you.

You set your own price. If you stumble, mumble and apologize, they figure there must be something wrong with you. Who should know better than you? If you brush it off as no big deal, they'll be happy to accept it that way, and probably forget it immediately, almost always by the time you've finished. If at the end they do remember, they'll be giving you high marks for handling it so well.

Blow In Their Ears And They'll Follow You Anywhere

Let's say you're *ready*. You feel *good* . You know your stuff, there's only one more speaker, and then: you're up. All right!

They introduce the next speaker and—DISASTER. She wows them! What do you do now? Well, whatever you do, don't compare yourself to other speakers.

A Toastmasters meeting provides a great example of how speakers can regulate the audience's mood. At this meeting, the first speaker gave a sensitive account of his weekend with his wife at a marriage encounter retreat. The experience affected him deeply and he had the audience in his palm. The next speaker gave an hilarious account of a real estate transaction that had everyone laughing.

Imagine yourself as that second speaker thinking, "Oh no. I can't give this lighthearted talk after his great speech."

Never compare yourself to any of the other speakers. Focus on your message and how it relates to the audience, and the audience will follow you anywhere.

Every day –

To Do

Practice not
inflating
my importance
so I can see
the big picture.

6

"Hey Look Me Over"

"How To Succeed In Business Without Really Trying"

Remember that the point of speaking isn't to showcase you.

The point is to share information.

Good speaking skills can boost your career. Learn to appreciate the importance of polishing your skills. Don't think you can avoid speaking opportunities and still get the same consideration for promotions.

Having better speaking skills will make you more useful to the company—good speakers can sell ideas faster and easier.

Looked at properly, knowing that good speaking skills are important can boost your career. Unfortunately, too many people don't use that knowledge properly— tending to focus on the possible negative career effects instead.

PEANUTS® By Charles M. Schulz

PEANUTS reprinted by permission of United Feature Syndicate, Inc.

Using that knowledge properly means appreciating the importance of polishing your skills. It means expecting to develop this skill the way you've learned so many others.

Remember the point—the apparent stated purpose of your speaking—is to get the information from you to them.

Look at giving a speech objectively—as though it were someone else's career involved, someone else's job, someone else's presentation. Look at the big picture.

And while you're at it, look at it as though you were going to be a member of the audience and had no responsibility in giving the presentation. Do this in plenty of time to avoid the pressure that builds as showtime approaches.

Perspective helps dissolve the shakes. If perception is reality, check out your perception.

"I Gotta Be Me"

Even habitually optimistic people see a half-empty glass when faced with giving a presentation—almost any presentation.

Here's one that presents a choice opportunity for losing your perspective: You're going to give a presentation to the BIG BOSS. Dread takes over as you imagine the infinite possibilities for failing, leaving little energy or time to actually prepare an effective presentation.

Someone had faith enough in you to give you your job. Someone thinks you have something to say. Remember some of your strengths here instead of digging up failings to focus on. Start at least with a half-full glass.

"I Fall To Pieces"

Your boss walks into the room during your talk. You hyperventilate while trying to continue talking. "What if I get something wrong?" "What if I don't say it the right way?" And on and on until you bury yourself.

Or you notice someone in your audience who knows more about the subject than you do, or has been with the company longer. "I know they're just waiting for me to make a mistake." "It isn't fair. Why aren't *they* giving the presentation."

Remember: Preparation alone isn't the key to eliminating nervousness. The key is beneath-the-surface focus. You won't be focused if you waste your time worrying about potential hazards.

It's true that if you do a good job, you'll make some points. It might even be true that if you don't do a good job, you could lose some. But count on this: If making points is what you think about, you'll be a sorry presenter.

"These Boots Are Gonna Walk All Over You"

But let's go over what you're thinking. You know Tom gets at least a little pleasure out of watching people squirm. He has arranged the room in which you're giving your presentation so that you're facing him and can't see most of the rest of your audience. He leans back in his chair with his feet up, looking down his nose without the trace of a smile as he asks you to tell him what happened this quarter.

You know he loves numbers and you know he loves to jump into the middle of presentations and question facts and conclusions. And you suspect that a couple of people you know haven't been promoted because they didn't do that well during a quarterly presentation.

BLONDIE   By Dean Young and Stan Drake

Reprinted with special permission of King Features Syndicate

With this bleak picture in mind, no wonder you're anxious. Let's take this depressing picture to its logical conclusion: Trying to avoid pitfalls sucks the life out of your natural style. You fall into a monotone, lose all your energy and enthusiasm, and stumble over information you know very well.

You have every right to recognize the danger in this situation, but you can't surrender to it. Tom will sense your fear and show no mercy. If you want to look good, reprogram your thinking.

It's a choice again. You can either choose to think of what you can lose, or choose to think of why the audience needs this information. If you let your mind dwell on company culture or politics, you're asking for trouble.

Your game plan:

- Organize your material around what matters to your audience

- Get interested in showing them how it affects the company and their jobs.

If, initially, you can't see how the information affects them, take the time to figure it out. When you do, you can honestly present it to them with the necessary conviction to focus them on the information, rather than on you.

"Set Yourself Free, Why Don't Ya Babe?"

Usually, the primary purpose of your presentation is to help your boss or your employees know what's going on. It's easy to think about the power bosses have over our lives. But, realistically, most executives are too busy to spend their time plotting employee humiliation schemes. They've got a company or a department to run, and you've got information they need.

Isn't that how you look at it when your employees report to you? Don't you have them report to you because you need to know what they've been doing? You need to know so you can coordinate what they've been doing with what the rest of the department is doing.

You appreciate concise, clear presentations. You appreciate it when employees don't make a big fuss or act uncomfortable. Your boss appreciates the same kind of presentation from you.

Presenting to those higher on the ladder suggests certain risks to us. Put it into perspective: You need information from your people, and your boss needs information from you.

Knowing this will set you free.

In the meantime-

Memo to me

The next time someone seems as though they're being critical of me, I'll practice choosing to give them the benefit of the doubt.

7

Think
Like
An
Audience

"It Takes Two, Baby—Me And You"

For most of us, it's a really novel concept, as the speaker, to imagine ourselves as an audience member. Yet it's important to spend a few totally unselfconscious moments thinking about how we would feel about this meeting, and this subject, if we were going to be on the receiving end.

To think like your audience, we need to take a little time to know something about them.

What are they interested in?

What is their point of view?

Are they going to have to make decisions based on what you tell them?

Are they going to have to report it to someone else? Do you need to win them over?

Are they old or young, educated or not, liberal or conservative?

If you don't know who they are, you won't be able to talk to them very well. Worse, they assume they're not very important to you.

BABY BLUES   by Jerry Scott & Rick Kirkman

Reprinted with special permission by King Features Syndicate

Two outside speakers at a management conference spoke on different aspects of a subject of vital interest to the audience, but both failed to link it to the work their audience was currently doing. What should have been fascinating was run-of-the-mill. These were generic speeches for any audience that wanted to know something about the speakers' subjects.

With very little effort, they could have employed examples and analogies specifically connected to this audience.

"Do Ya Love Me?"

So when you're the designated speaker, for your own protection, continue to think like an audience.

When you're in the audience, you know what you like and don't like. Just because you're the speaker doesn't mean you've lost that insight.

Sometimes, because there's been so much hype about the occasion or the speaker, you may be unsure of your judgment; it's rather like the Emperor's New Clothes: We keep wondering what we're missing because "it doesn't seem that good to me." You can usually trust your instincts (unless you're being influenced by a personal prejudice).

If we intuitively know good from bad, interesting from boring when we're in the audience, why do we do the same boring things when we're the speaker? Probably because we forget it's not about us. We forget to sit in the audience's seat. Business audiences are used to being bored, so they aren't that surprised when you bore them. That doesn't mean they won't be thrilled if you don't.

Do everyone a favor. Take pity on your audience.

● ●

Surprise Your Audience: Choose to be interesting.

● ●

"You've Got The Magic Touch"

We love speakers who are animated and interested because it makes them interesting. It's great when we find one who uses good analogies, interesting visuals, a different approach. We wonder why everyone can't be like that—it's so much easier to listen. And we remember more.

But when it's our turn to speak, we play it safe. Now, it's true that initially it takes more time to be creative. And it's riskier. You know everyone else has survived the "old" way, and you've managed to keep your job with the same old stuff, so why bother changing?

Don had to give a presentation to an industry conference and wanted to try something new, based on what he'd learned in our seminar. He broke with industry tradition, as well as his own, and used a few simple visuals and graphic examples. He used no notes. He won the hearts of his audience, and had a great time.

Being more interesting and creative doesn't have to be risky; you should never do anything inappropriate for your audience. But we audiences would love not to have to work so hard, and not to be bored. Creativity doesn't even have to take a lot more time (once you get into a different frame of mind). Taking pity on the audience will put you in touch with your creativity, and that doesn't have to take any longer.

Creating interesting visuals can consume more time, depending on what technology and support staff you have available. But there is usually a way to have more effective visuals without devoting your life to them.

We'll talk more about that later. For right now, this is all part of thinking of how you like to be treated as an audience—having the information presented in an interesting way—and that involves both creative thinking and a willingness to change.

"Honesty Is Such A Lonely Word"

The meaning of life, I'll leave to someone else. The method of life is selling. Good salespeople are good because they've learned to think like their audience (their buyer). Selling is helping; speaking is selling.

Selling ideas is your job, whether or not it's in your job description. Children are born selling—this movie, that shirt, those shoes, this party.

Selling is about the buyer's point of view. You don't sell your family on a vacation in the mountains because you like fishing. You don't sell your kids on eating their vegetables because vegetables are good for them. You don't sell your boss on giving you a raise because you want one.

You may protest, "I'm not in sales. I could never be a salesperson, not me." Because deep down we equate "salesperson" with playwright Arthur Miller's beleaguered salesman, Willie Loman. What is the sales stereotype? Plaid jacket, fast talker, slick. No matter how many real salespeople we work with, unfortunately, that's the stereotype—someone trying to fast-talk us into buying.

When someone new to a sales force tells you, "I'm not really a salesperson," they're apologizing for themselves, thinking that's a liability. Unfortunately, that person has bought into the stereotype, too. In fact, they've been recruited to sales because they're genuine; they try to help clients solve problems instead of trying to follow a script.

Genuine sells. Slick doesn't. If slick is successful, it's short-term. Genuinely caring for your audience (your customer) creates (or sustains) a relationship that makes selling possible.

The kid at the door trying to sell magazine subscription so he can go to camp is ignoring what's in it for the audience. Buying a magazine so he can go to camp isn't an incentive for me—unless it keeps him from bothering me all summer. Now there's an incentive!

Sell me on a magazine because I'll love it. Sell me on a vacation because of how much fun I'll have. Sell me on eating my vegetables because it will make me grow up to look like Wonder Woman. Sell me on giving you a raise because of your value in achieving department goals.

What does this have to do with speaking? Speaking is selling ideas. And selling is about developing relationships. Be genuine; pay attention to your relationship with your audience, and captivate them.

"Put A Little Love In Your Heart"

Connecting with your audience helps you accomplish your mission. Acknowledge me and validate my concerns if you want me to consider yours.

Israeli prime minister, Yitzhak Rabin, speaking in Washington at the signing of the Israeli-Palestinian Declaration of Principles in September 1993, had to connect with several distinctly different audiences, many of whom objected to this historic declaration.

He reached out first to the Israelis by validating their pain: "It is certainly not easy for the families of the victims of the wars, violence, terror, whose pain will never heal . . . . For them, this ceremony has come too late. Today . . . we remember each and every one of them with everlasting love."

He then reached out to the Palestinians: "Let me say to you, the Palestinians, we are destined to live together on the same soil in the same land.

"We, the soldiers who have returned from battles stained with blood; . . . we who have come from a land where parents bury their children; we who have fought against you, the Palestinians, we say to you today in a loud and clear voice: Enough of blood and tears.

"Enough! We have no desire for revenge; we harbor no hatred toward you. We, like you, are people—people who want to build a home, to plant a tree, to love, live side by side with you in dignity, in affinity, as human beings, as free men."

Thinking like an audience means connecting with your common humanity.

Not every subject is as emotional as Prime Minister Rabin's speech. But every presentation affects people in some way; there is some human connection.

You can make me care about your statistics. Just make them real to me and relevant to my life. Statistics show something about *people*. You may have to step back to see the connection, but it's there.

Use life examples to connect your point to me.

Be real, look at the subject from my point of view, work on our relationship. The sale's not guaranteed, but at least I'll be listening to you—and that's the first step.

"I Got Rhythm . . . . Who Could Ask for Anything More?"

Connecting with the audience means getting into their rhythm. For a good example of getting into the rhythm, watch kids on a playground waiting to enter the ropes when jumping double-dutch jump rope. They don't want to get tangled in the ropes.

Driving in New York City is a good place to understand rhythm, too; your fenders will be safer if you go with the flow.

In speaking, if you want your message and your ego to stay intact, get into the rhythm of the idea, explore your audience, *listen* (focus on what's going on outside you, not on yourself).

Analyzing your audience while you're preparing your presentation is part of getting into their rhythm. Mingling with them before you present, talking, finding out what's happened recently that affects them, is part of it, too. Get out of yourself and listen to them. This isn't about you.

Kevin was amazing. He told us we were supposed to be the actual audience that he was to speak to at work the following week. He got out of himself and into the rhythm of his intended audience and the importance of their knowing this information. It was beautiful. The class was ready to do anything he wanted.

I've seen motivational speakers irritate the audience by bringing their own rhythm, having no sense of how the audience feels about being asked to do cheerleader yells at 8 o'clock in the morning with a stranger.

When you get into your audience's rhythm, you're invisible because you're part of the occasion. Everything fits. When you insist on your own rhythm, there's cacophony. You know cacophony. That's when you insist on taking the rhythm of your mom's house into your mother-in-law's house.

"Don't Go Changing To Try To Please Me"

But most important, it's the rhythm of the idea you're respecting, not your rhythm or theirs. If the audience is angry or depressed, don't turn over the keys. Be aware of their rhythm, respect it, but don't surrender.

If your audience is angry because of a new employee policy, don't start out defensively or angrily if you want to communicate with them. However, knowing what the mood is should help you figure out how to connect with them. Understanding their perspective can help you move into those jump ropes without getting tangled in them.

Calm, deliberate movements, a quiet firm voice— or quick, agitated movements and a harsh voice. The latter probably matches their rhythm, and escalates it.

The former recognizes their state of mind and the need to treat them as reasonable people who deserve a hearing.

To know what their rhythm is, you have to stop thinking about yourself and see how best to communicate with them given their frame of mind, whether it's upbeat, angry, neutral, or sad.

Former President Ronald Reagan often caught the mood of the nation in his speeches, recognized it and went with it or changed it through humor. At times of tragedy, he moved with the mood, showed he shared our feelings, and offered hope. His brief tribute to the team who died on the Challenger space shuttle was a prime example. "Today is a day for mourning and remembering," he began. Then he proceeded to name all seven victims of the explosion. It was a simple, human, moving speech.

Every occasion, every subject, every audience has its own rhythm. You can tap into it only if you get out of yourself and get into what's going on outside you. If the company just won the big contract, your audience is going to have a different rhythm than if they just got word of massive layoffs.

Technically Speaking

Technical audiences have a rhythm, too, and it's not nearly as stiff as their stereotype. Techies are people, too. And, technically speaking, technical speaking shouldn't be so technical.

If you're a techno-whiz speaking to other technical folks, apply some of that skill and logical thinking to figure out how you can make your report more interesting. It's possible to lighten up a bit and still have a little R-E-S-P-E-C-T.

Technical speakers are uncompromising with the material they deliver, worrying that they'll lose credibility with the audience if they aren't dry and detailed. "My audience is full of engineers; they're used to getting this kind of detail delivered in college classes. They'll think we're talking down to them if we make it conversational. They want lots of details and they hate writing it down."

Granted, all that may be true, but you probably have some latitude between what you're presenting now and what would be considered simplistic, before losing their attention or your credibility. If your presentations could use some improving, consider how you can deliver enough information to accomplish your purpose and theirs without using crowded slides and nonstop technical jargon. And consider giving them the details in your handouts.

Techies are pretty funny people (maybe humorous would be a better choice of words). "Humorous" and "bright" shouldn't translate into boring presentations.

One way to liven up a presentation is to relate numbers and data to familiar items. Edward D. Young III vice president external affairs and associate general counsel for Bell Atlantic, gave some stats this way: "The Intel 486 microprocessor . . . weighs less than a packet of Sweet 'n Low, uses less than two watts of electricity, and processes 54 million instructions per second . . . . The average consumer today has more computing power in his or her wristwatch than existed in the entire world before 1961."

• •

Techies are people, too.

• •

Lightening up a presentation doesn't mean being condescending or simplistic. And it won't make you look unqualified. To make a difficult subject seem easy, you have to understand it. A friend of mine goes so far as to say, "If you can't explain it in 6-year-old terms, you don't understand it."

Staying in the abstract and using all the familiar jargon acts as a substitute for getting under the skin of the subject. It takes less understanding of the subject to do that than it does to talk conversationally about it.

When you're talking to nontechnical audiences, think how you would explain the material to a bright high school student—they're smart enough to understand the subject, but have insufficient context.

When talking to technical people, have a little fun with your approach so they can too. Get creative. As a

Mammoth Lakes billboard said, "Raise your expectations a few thousand feet."

Be simple, conversational, and interesting.

Bonus benefit: You'll be able to remember most of your presentation without needing notes, allowing you more freedom to connect with your audience.

"Lullaby And Goodnight"

There's no such thing as a boring subject, only bored speakers, who then are boring—and the subject gets blamed.

The audience won't be interested unless you are. (Crucial: not just interested, but interested at the moment of delivery. Be there.) We'd rather listen to someone who's fired up.

"Fired up," you say? "Wait a minute! I'm giving the annual budget report. It's just numbers. It's boring. How can you expect me to get fired up about numbers?"

"It's only the monthly safety inspection information—same stuff every month."

"How do you expect me to be on fire when I explain the differences in the HMO plans?"

A question: If it's that boring, why are you giving it? Save everyone's time and e-mail it to them. If it bores you, what hope does your audience have? They're

CALVIN AND HOBBES   By Bill Watterson

trapped. No way to escape and forced to sit there while you do penance. It's clearly a waste of time, except for the one or two who really want the information because it directly affects their jobs.

But wait a minute! Why are numbers boring? Granted, "2" by itself doesn't move me. But your report probably doesn't consist of just a lot of "2's" or "645's." What you put with those numbers makes the difference —two hot-fudge sundaes, or losing two clients, or saving $645 a week on purchasing costs.

Sales are up? That's great news! Sales are down? Ouch! We need to know so we can make decisions. Budget's increased? Decreased? What does that mean to me? How does that affect my job? My department? The company's future?

Numbers are energizing—when they're connected to something that matters to your audience. Then it'll be easy to smolder some (even if you don't totally ignite).

When Your Number Is Up

Any report that includes naked numbers and facts sounds real technical to most audiences. And although you personally love every number and fact (it took a long time to pull it all together), experience tells you your audience won't.

Here's part of Andy Rooney's explanation of the federal deficit. "Say you're a kid 8 years old whose parents give you an allowance of $1 a week, or $52 a year. If you operate the way the federal government does, you'll spend one-third more than your allowance, or about $69.

"Next year, they estimate the federal deficit will rise even higher. If you're a kid, you'll be spending more like $84 after only getting a $52 allowance."

The proportions are the same, and give a clear sense of the idea involved without the encumbrance of the actual numbers. Once the concept is understood, or the direction of the findings is clear, rounded-off versions of the actual numbers are easier to take in.

Give the big picture first (in words and in visuals). That may be all you need, that and a handout with the details. If you need to say more, the audience has the context to deal with it.

"Oh, Won't You Stay, Just A Little Bit Longer"

Whatever your audience, whatever your presentation, you have to overcome the last temptation. You've made it past the shoals of split focus, you've cleared the rocks of possible confrontation, and the last few words are in sight. Yahoo! You made it.

Not just yet.

You're thinking about yourself again. Instead, remember the words of that famous philosopher, Yogi Berra: "It ain't over till it's over." To send your message home, you have to stay invisible, stay focused on the message. All your energy, all your focus, all your interest must be riveted on your target.

To be invisible, stand still for a few seconds and think about what you've just said. Don't be thinking, "Oh boy, I'm finished!" That will scatter the moment and draw attention to yourself.

• •

Stick the landing — just like gymnastics

• •

Most golf and tennis instructors harp on follow-through—stay with the movement until it's complete. In your presentation, you're not through till you're clean out of sight of everyone in that room.

When you get in your car is a good time to relax and feel finished.

Terry finished a moving story about escaping from Vietnam as a child with his theme, "You can reach your dream." He stood absolutely still for a few moments as he held onto that thought. The audience was motionless, absorbed in his message.

As you finish:

Plant your feet.

Focus.

Deliver the closing with total commitment.

Stay focused on those closing words and the message they contain, letting them reverberate within you. Release the thought gently when you have finished appreciating it. Then move off. Powerful. Effective.

It ain't over till it's over. And over isn't until you're completely out of sight of your audience. Stay focused on helping the audience and don't steal a moment for yourself until then.

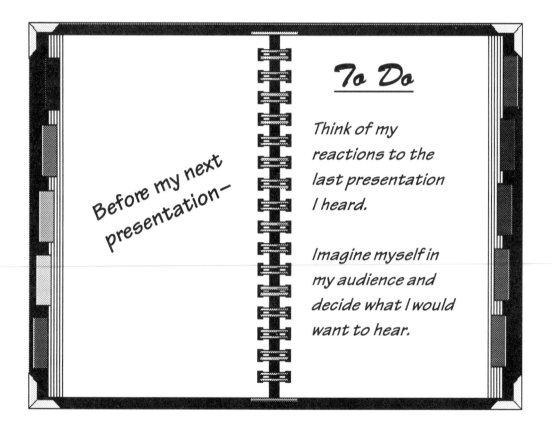

8

"Going Out Of My Head Over You"

"One Is The Loneliest Number," Part I

Speaking is a mind game; you want to be sure you're playing on the right team. Your audience is part of your team; thinking of them that way will help you be in your right mind.

Instead, when you're up in front, you feel totally, miserably alone. That's in your mind, not theirs (unless there's hostility built into the occasion.) They'll be with you all the way—if you let them. Most audiences are friendly, or friendly to neutral. They're willing to accept you.

As you stand there, think of yourself as one of the group. Consider them as friends you haven't met yet. Remember they're human. Most people want to be liked (including those in your audience), and they respond to you based on your attitude, friendly or aloof.

Give them a chance to like you—like them first. In this game, you always get to make the first move. This isn't about you. It's about them.

"One Is The Loneliest Number," Part 2

Same game, other side of the coin. Some people don't feel alone when they're in front of an audience; they feel like a star in front of the adoring crowds. What makes these people feel uncomfortable is conversing with just one other person.

Why? Because in speaking to an audience, you can perfect your message and your timing, you can release energy, you can enjoy the thrill of people laughing and applauding. It's a great ego boost, and darn fun! For these folks the hard part is talking to the audience members afterwards.

I've seen some fine speakers work the audience with skill and understanding then change completely when talking to people afterwards. All the warmth and naturalness they displayed on the platform disappeared. They appear to love humanity in the aggregate, rather than individually. (This can also be caused by thinking the speech is over when you give your closing. You mentally shut down and have no energy left for talking to anyone. That can be cured by remembering "It ain't over till it's over.")

In front of a crowd, there's none of that messy interaction stuff that's required talking one-on-one. No responses are needed. No understanding of that individual. No personal connecting. No listening. Some who love being "on stage" are not so afraid of making a mistake in a speech as in an unscripted conversation.

It's what you think about a situation that makes it so. Some think an audience is going to discover their flaws. Others think an individual will.

If this sounds like you (preferring to speak to audiences rather than individuals) analyze what's taking place when you're so comfortable in front of that audience. You're probably focused on the message and not thinking about whether or not they like you. You have something to say, and that's all that matters.

In a conversation, it's the same principle: Don't think about whether or not they like you, just focus on the big picture. Think: What does this person need, what can I tell her that will be useful? This doesn't mean having to bare your soul (something that would no doubt make them uncomfortable), or losing your privacy. It means looking at the situation from the listener's point-of-view.

It's two sides of the same coin: An audience cares about how your speech affects *them*, whether it's an audience of one or one thousand. They're not thinking about you; they're thinking about themselves.

Take the same mind set when you're talking to one person and you'll learn to get the same result.

"Waiting To Exhale"

Whether it's giving a speech, angling for a date, or having an uncomfortable conversation, you're familiar with the rush. You know it. That feeling when you're suddenly aware of being on the spot—the rapid heartbeat, the "fight or flight" syndrome.

Don't surrender. Resist it. Be still and get control of yourself. Focus on an object or focus inwardly while you breathe. Breathe and inventory your body — plant your feet, quiet your hands and your mind, breathe your heart rate down. Beat the rush. And then, wrap your brain around what you want to say.

For best results, don't wait until your foot is in your mouth, or your mind has crashed. Before saying the first word, take as much time as you need to synchronize your mind and mouth. It's worth it.

"Fight or flight" implies danger. Stop thinking that speaking to an audience is dangerous so your body won't be tricked into preparing for battle.

The "rush" isn't necessary if it's from fear. A shot of adrenalin is great. Adrenalin kicks in when you're looking forward to something you enjoy; it isn't wedded to pain. You don't have to be nervous, and you can have more fun if you're not.

"I Shall Never Breathe Again"

Repeat after me: Breathing is good.

Right before a presentation, there's way too much to do and to think about, so we neglect proper breathing. Bad move. Keep breathing. In with the good air, out with the bad. All that good air, taken in evenly, rhythmically and quietly will help release the tension. It slows your heart to a more normal rate. It clears your mind and permits clear thought.

Focus totally on your breathing for a few moments (or minutes, even—whatever you need). Count the breaths. Time them. Feel the air coming and going.

In addition to saving your life, it also saves your voice, or gives you one. Nice relaxed total body breathing supports your voice by starting way down in your body, not up in your chest, throat or nose.

To get the idea, lie on your back, put a book on your abdomen and just relax. As you breathe, the book will show you the way you breathe naturally so you can recognize proper breathing when you're standing up.

KEEP BREATHING

Remember: Breathing is good.

"It's Been A Hard Day's Night"

If your mind plays tricks on you during a presentation, you're probably not immune to the tricks it plays beforehand—like the night before.

Oh, those sleepless nights. Your presentation is tomorrow. You desperately want to sleep so you'll be fresh for it; or at least so you can stop stressing out for a while. But no. Those words just go round and round in your head.

To regain your sanity, you need to regroup, take control, and get off the mental merry-go-round. Ruminating ruins rhetoric (and a good night's sleep.) Rehearsing your speech in bed is counterproductive. Your brain doesn't function the same when it's lying down, so rehearsing in bed won't help when you're standing up to present.

Think about something else. Easier said than done, you say? Get up and read "Murder at the Vicarage." Iron your shirt. Or, sincerely think about what you're offering the audience. Look at the big picture. Pretend the assignment belongs to someone else. Picture yourself sitting in the audience anticipating the speaker. What do you hope to find out? You'll do yourself more good analyzing the purpose and the need than you will going over and over the words (or over and over the anxiety).

Or you could recall your boss's last speech in excruciating detail. That might work better than Sominex.

"To Sleep, Perchance To Dream"

You've lived through the night, you're fresh and focused. As you talk, you're looking at people to connect with them, to converse with them, to encourage them, to see if you're on the same wavelength. It maintains the energy level—yours and theirs.

But wait! That person's not looking at me! Oh no! He's sleeping. What do I do now?

First, keep your wits about you and don't take it personally. See if it's a general problem, or if it's just one person. One person is no big deal. Late night (you know how hard it can be to get to sleep sometimes). Sleeping sickness. Short attention span.

On the other hand, if they're all nodding off, you better ask yourself some questions. Take inventory to figure out what isn't working. Your first question might be, "Am I interested in what I'm saying, or have I gone on auto pilot?" Refresh your own interest.

This is one of those places to use that definition of listening—get "tuned in to what's going on outside and not on yourself." Those ideas Henry Ford spoke of are knocking on your head trying to get in. Listen with the idea of solving a problem. Not your problem, *a* problem.

Have you taken a break recently? Could you use a change of pace—ask the audience some questions, let them ask you questions, or give them a problem to solve? Or maybe the room is too warm (or cold) or there isn't any air circulating.

Whatever's wrong, take time to fix it. And don't take it personally. If you do, you may race through to limit your embarrassment. Finishing isn't your primary goal—you're supposed to be helping the audience.

"This Is The Dawning Of The Age Of Aquarius"

Whatever the reason, feeling personal about *anything* in your presentation calls for strong measures. Imagining your audience naked isn't one of them. Forget it. You don't need mind games here.

SALLY FORTH By Greg Howard and Craig Macintosh

Reprinted with special permission of King Features Syndicate

Imagining them in their underwear (or speculating on the construction of their navels) is just a gimmick to shift your focus off your perceived inadequacy onto theirs. Playing that game assumes you are deficient, and that you need to trick yourself into feeling competent enough to face them.

That certainly is one way to get you to realize that they are people, regular people with regular lives families, children, hobbies, failings, etc. But there's a down side. What if your imagination runs away and you get distracted by what you imagine? Oops!

It's better to stay focused on presenting your material and being invisible, rather than something so potentially dangerous. Take the high road.

Yes, an audience has an agenda, and it's helpful to recognize that it centers around what's going to happen to them during the program. You have definite opinions when you're in the audience, but you're usually not focusing on the things the speaker thinks you're focusing on. You're wondering "What's in it for me?" And that's what your audience is wondering. If you do the "naked" thing, you won't be able to focus on telling them.

"I've Got The World On A String"

When you've got the world on a string, you can do no wrong—everybody loves you, everyone wants to buy, everybody is your friend. You don't need mind games to win the day.

If you've got a new suit, a great hair cut, just won a prize, or gotten a promotion, you feel "hot." And when you feel "hot" there's a spring in your step, a glint in your eye, a spark in your voice, and people respond favorably—they respond to what you're feeling about you.

Think about it a moment. How do you feel when you're applying for a job you don't need? Smooth? Or negotiating for a car you haven't set your heart on? In control? You're loose. You feel good. You're on a roll. You're like a political candidate who's way ahead in the polls.

Compare that to how you feel when you're going after business you desperately need. Or your heart is set on that car, or that painting.

Feel the difference? Do you remember how the other person reacts to you? Others take their cue from you. You set your own price. When you're confident people respond quite differently to your message than when they sense that you're insecure or desperate.

Sarah began presenting her show "Off Broadway." That is, she'd make appointments with clients she didn't think she could sell to, or those she didn't care if she could get. Minus the pressure of needing to make the sale, she gave such great presentations she actually sold some of them. And it gave her great confidence when she started "On Broadway."

When you feel like you've got the world on a string, you're invincible—you get the date, make the sale, sink the putt. Which approach do you use when you're speaking—world on a string (winner) or perennial victim (loser)? Which one is you in front of an audience? Hmmm? Get the drift?

Step out with confidence; you've got nothing to lose.

"Commit The Crime And Do The Time"

Speaking shouldn't generate victims. Avoid the crime: Stop seeing yourself as a victim, or you'll do the time—and serve your sentence in front of your audience (it feels like a life sentence).

Act like a victim, you'll get mugged—metaphorically speaking, of course. An audience doesn't respect a speaker who feels (and consequently acts) like a victim.

There shouldn't be any victims here and it's up to you to make sure there aren't, so try this: pity your poor audience—they could be the victims. They're at your mercy. They don't have to listen, but they feel obliged to stay in their seats. Don't make them victims of poorly arranged content and dull delivery.

Remember: There is no such thing as a boring subject.

Reduce the crime rate. Turn the search light on the idea.

Before my next presentation—

To Do

Before I say anything, I will breathe a moment, recognize these are people, human beings, and focus on what I want to say to them.

9

"Interview With The Vampire"

"Trouble Right Here In River City"

If your business offends large segments of the population, you may really feel like a victim, a lamb being lead to slaughter, when you have to appear in public. Do yourself a favor by learning how to make your audience less hostile.

Your best weapon with a hostile audience is to have nothing up your sleeve, to be someone they can feel comfortable talking with. That doesn't mean smothering them with your personality—it's connecting with them, developing a relationship. You're the seller. They're your prospect.

Visualizing their hostility fans your fear, and what you expect in the way of trouble is what you get—and then some. Your defenses go up (yes, it's obvious to them), and now you are a target. You either look angry, evasive (shifty maybe?), or just plain nervous.

California Assemblyman Larry Bowler of Elk Grove and Assemblywoman Sheila Kuehl of Santa Monica are on opposite sides of the political fence on a myriad of issues. He's pro-gun, she supports gun control. He's pro-death penalty, she is not. Bowler says, "I can talk to Sheila. We disagree philosophically, but she's reasonable."

In an article in the *Los Angeles Times*, Kuehl said she "takes pains to be friendly with everyone and never burns a bridge." According to the article, the result is relationships with all parts of the political spectrum, and cooperation on bills.

The more unapproachable you are, the easier it is to pick on you because you're not one of them; they don't feel responsible for an outsider's well-being. On the other hand, the more they feel you have something in common, the more polite they're inclined to be. So your best bet is to try to make friends.

You're thinking: That's easy for you to say. I'm the one facing the attack. Those people are out for blood—mine!

"Easier Said Than Done"

I didn't say it was easy. But it works. If you look belligerent, frightened or aloof, you're inviting them to attack. Perhaps you've tried any or all of those attitudes and know how painful they can be. They come from taking yourself too seriously. Your hope lies in seeing the problem from the audience's point of view, not taking their anger personally, and looking for areas of agreement and ways to resolve the issue—not for a way you can win.

Albert had to meet with employees of each division of their company to explain how reorganizing was going to affect them. And it clearly was going to affect them—hundreds of jobs were being eliminated. And they were clearly a hostile audience whose anger was directed at the symbol of the company: Albert.

What Albert realized he needed was to acknowledge to himself that the new policy, while necessary, was creating pain for his audience.

Often, the speaker feels so terrible about what's happened he puts up a businesslike front trying to keep the emotion out of it, thinking that is the safest, best way to handle it. The audience, in turn, sees a cold, uncaring villain, and their anger escalates.

Remember this: Your audience will benefit from the information you have to offer. You are giving them information they need in order to make decisions about their lives.

Another good way to defuse hostility is to use humor. When JFK was rumored to be buying votes, he responded by reading to the press a telegram ostensibly from his father: "Jack: Don't buy a single vote more than is necessary. I'll be damned if I'm going to pay for a landslide."

Again, when he appointed his brother Robert (who had no practical experience as an attorney after law school) as Attorney General, JFK quieted the resulting furor with the observation "I see nothing wrong with giving Robert some legal experience as attorney general before he goes out to practice law."

Ronald Reagan brushed aside the potential roadblock posed by his age by remarking in the presidential debates with Walter Mondale, " . . . And I want you to know that I will not make age an issue of this campaign. I am not going to exploit for political purposes my opponent's youth and inexperience." Even Mondale grinned broadly—which was the only appropriate response.

Hostility sometimes surfaces in the form of questions during a presentation. If people are genuinely in pain, or are fearful, listen with compassion to their remarks. Respond genuinely to their concern before offering another perspective.

If someone is being a jerk, don't take it personally. If he's looking for a forum, you may need to give him a temporary one until you've found a way to get him to stop.

In any event, be caring. If you're not, the rest of the audience will turn on you. Remember, you're there to build relationships.

That's Why They Make Vanilla And Chocolate

Someone is going to disagree with your point of view. Count on it. So don't be surprised if they express it in front of a group you're talking to.

Don't take it personally. You're both entitled to your own opinion—even if one of you is wrong. That's why they make vanilla and chocolate. Various points of view help keep people honest and encourage creativity.

Give your "opponent" a break. He may need some attention today.

Of course, if you've made friends with the audience, they'll be less inclined to want to make you look bad. Disarm them. Make friends right at the start.

What Would Miss Manners Say?

Inconsiderate behavior isn't usually as incapacitating as hostility, but side conversations can really be annoying whether they're during a presentation or in a meeting. They're almost always distracting and, if you don't do something, they'll definitely become annoying.

The more annoyed you let yourself be, the less effective your presentation gets. So you have to do something. Part of the aggravation stems from the potential threat to your leadership.

First, deal with yourself: Don't allow yourself to get flustered or angry. You're bound to discomfit or alienate your audience if you lose your cool.

Second, deal with the problem. If you're not angry or nervous, you'll be able to think clearly, and then you can decide what to do. Maybe a well-placed pause will be enough silence to get them to stop themselves. (During the pause, you need to be thinking about your message, not focused on waiting for them to be quiet.)

Maybe it seems right to say something. Just be sure what you say feels like it came to you from a divine source. If you say something snide to the talkers, your audience (who a minute ago was annoyed by the talkers) will turn against you. You've attacked one of their own. You've just magnified your problem.

· ·

Controlling the meeting is a matter of not feeling out of control.

· ·

Well, what if pausing doesn't work? Get the talkers' attention without being obvious, or at least without being unkind. You might move to some other part of the stage, or room—the movement may catch their attention. Or, non-judgmentally moving closer to them would draw more attention their way and help them wake up to what they're doing.

Sometimes you can involve the audience right then by asking a question. Once I just looked at the whole area of the room and asked, "Can you all hear this okay?" Maybe you can ask a question that specifically relates to the talkers, something they know the answer to. Involving the audience shifts the focus in the room and creates a different atmosphere.

"Have any of you had experience with this?" "Could somebody back me up with an example from your department?" If you're sure somebody has, you can mention a couple of names to give more focus to the question, and more attention to the audience. In this case, bringing in some other voices can be enough change to stop the side discussion.

When you're leading a meeting, or making a presentation, the audience depends on you to keep it moving, keep it interesting and keep it in order. If you want to feel good about your performance and look good to the audience, accept the responsibility, but don't take it personally.

Because you're dealing with people (people being what they are), it's quite a challenge. With enough yanks on that choke chain, you can triumph.

In the meantime—

To Do

Practice not taking things personally so hostility and rudeness won't throw me off balance in a presentation.

I can practice with my boss, my family, or a rude clerk.

MANAGING YOUR BODY

WHAT THE MIND CAN CONCEIVE
THE BODY CAN ACHIEVE

Sweating it out while part of you runs out the door

10

"Don't Fence Me In"

"I'm A Wanderer"

If you ever want to see grownups cry, tell them they have to stand still while speaking. Guaranteed for at least some good whining.

"Standing still is boring."

"Moving keeps the audience interested."

"Besides, I can't stand still."

Everyone's a mover and shaker; they want to walk (read: pace) while they talk. They passionately argue they're more effective when they move around.

Maybe. Usually not. It's more likely pent-up energy randomly escaping.

When you're keyed up, pacing is the easiest thing to do, but not the most effective.

If you want to command more attention, stand vigorously still. Or move with purpose. In this way, you allow your audience to concentrate on what you're saying, and they're more likely to believe you because you seem solid and confident.

At a recent three-hour seminar, the speaker paced constantly the entire three hours! Three steps in this direction, four in that. It wasn't energizing; it was frustrating, irritating, and exhausting. Someone must have mentioned it to him in the past because he brought it up, commenting, rather defensively, that this was his style.

If you can't give a talk without walking around, your body is in control. And that means you're in trouble.

Solution: Stand still until you can do so without thinking about it. It's easier than you think. Before starting, e-mail your feet, "Stay." Then give your talk without thinking about them. Once you can stand still, it's okay to move.

The rule for walking is the same as for getting a bank loan—if you don't need it, you can have it. It's also the rule for notes: once you don't feel dependent on them, you can have them.

"Take A Walk On The Wild Side"

Bill Clinton, during the televised presidential debates with then-President Bush and businessman Ross Perot, was the only one to come out from behind the lectern. He moved purposefully to the audience and spoke directly to them. He stood still as he spoke. And he won the election.

Try something really wild. Stand still and use all that dynamic energy to inspire and excite the audience about your subject, attracting them to it via expressive gestures and facial expressions, vivid words said with conviction.

"Let's Get Physical"

Well, getting control of your feet doesn't spell the end of it: you've still got hands. For most people, the worst moment comes when they realize that two very large objects have suddenly appeared at the end of their wrists. And they have to be managed, somehow, for the duration of the presentation.

Hands pretty well take care of themselves when you're not thinking about them; they're usually fine during conversations. It's thinking about them that makes them unruly. My suggestion: When you don't know what to do with your hands, just let them hang quietly at your sides. At first, it feels awkward, but it looks composed, and solves the immediate problem: "Where did these come from, and what should I do with them?"

You don't need to leave them at your sides, but it's a great fall-back position when you don't know what else to do. Or you can let them rest at waist level; either works as a home base. Both places are definitely better than the "fig-leaf," hands in pockets, or crossed arms. The rest of the time you can use them to help you tell your story.

Illustrate your point using your hands and arms as you do in conversation. Spontaneous, appropriate gestures make great visual aids. Random waving, or keeping time with your words distracts everyone. The range of gestures is determined by the setting; when you're in front of a group you have more space than you do one-on-one, so you can use bigger gestures. If you think using little ones won't draw attention to yourself—think again.

...THIS PROJECT WILL BE HUGE

One woman unintentionally gave the class a giggle as she described waiting for the train to cross. With her arms pinned to her sides, she gestured with only her hand to illustrate the train's passing. The tiny movement fluttering against her thigh looked ridiculous.

It's distracting when:

- Your hands gesture separately from your arms, that is, bending only at the wrists.

- Your hands keep time with your words.

- You use the same gesture over and over.

- Your arms hang at your sides but your hands flap. This gives the effect of imminent take-off.

- You're talking about something huge, and your arms don't stretch to their full length.

- You keep your elbows glued to your sides.

Gestures need to match what you're talking about: big ideas call for big gestures, little for little. Think about what you're saying, and they'll happen naturally.

"Take My Arms, I Want To Lose Them"

Fear of losing a limb seems to be a big problem. Many a good gesture self-destructs because it's not allowed its appropriate life span. Leave it in the air till you're through with the thought. Then quietly release it.

Richard Nixon often pulled his gestures "home" too quickly, which drew attention to his personality rather than keeping it focused on what he said. His "staccato" gestures added to a tense image.

A good gesture almost never involves equal energy on the outward thrust and the release. It's more like the energy used in rowing—dig in/release.

"Fly Me To The Moon"

This doesn't mean you have to gesture when you talk. You do have to keep from fidgeting. President Nixon was actually more effective when he wasn't gesturing because his gestures were so tense and unnatural they worked against what he was saying most of the time.

Solid, purposeful gestures can help focus you and your audience, and keep you from fidgeting—that is, releasing that extra energy inappropriately.

The more comfortable you get, the more likely your hands are to correlate with your thoughts. They're a team. Ignore your hands while you're talking. Don't *try* to gesture. If they move, fine. If you notice them fidgeting, stop.

"I Can't Get Started With You"

Practice your speech once, silently. Stand up, plant your feet, and say your speech in your head. As you process the ideas, experiment with how you can support your message with your arms, hands and body.

Try out a lot of gestures—big ones. You'll loosen up your arms and your brain. Don't hold back worrying that you can't use that many, or that they can't be that large, or that it doesn't feel natural. A little arm-swinging will begin to make them feel natural. (Haven't you always wanted to be a swinger?)

"Know When To Hold 'Em, Know When To Fold 'Em"

What about those people who tell you you shouldn't use your hands when you talk? They just may be wrong. That advice is often given by people who heard someone else say it.

Gestures can be some of your best visuals. So the truth is: If they're supporting what you say, good. They help make you invisible. If they're distracting people from the ideas, they've gotta go. Bouncing, waving, keeping time with your words, all fall in that category.

You don't need to stop "talking with your hands." You just need to be sure they're saying the same thing your mouth is saying. Ask a friend who will tell you the truth, and who has good judgment, to tell you if your hands are distracting, or watch yourself on video (and be kind to yourself).

Watch other people's gestures for awhile and it will all come together for you. Tim Galwey in "The Inner Game of Tennis" says your tennis game will be improved for a couple of weeks after watching a championship tennis tournament. The same can be true when you see a good speaker. You get in the rhythm.

FOR BETTER OR FOR WORSE   By Lynn Johnston

"Yeah, Yeah, Yeah"

Are you afflicted with verbal fillers? Don't despair. It doesn't take much time to get rid of them. "Ah," "and uh," "you know" and "like" are habits you've developed. You have to be aware of what you're doing before you can stop.

Filling in the pauses with sound keeps people from thinking about your last words. Punctuating your thoughts with nonsense words is, you know, distracting, and, like, makes you look unprofessional. You know?

Part of the solution: getting over yourself. When you stop thinking about what can happen to you as a result of this presentation, you'll be aware of what your body is doing and saying. So you're more likely to hear those fillers.

Sterner measures: Ask someone to tell you every time you use a fillers in regular conversation. With that kind of personal coaching, it won't take long to stop using them. Realize up front that it's darn annoying to be interrupted while you're talking, and don't take it out on your helper. You asked for it. Appreciate the favor.

"The Way I Walk Is Just The Way I Walk"

So this is what they mean about being able to walk and chew gum. You have to talk without fillers, maneuver your body, AND remember what you want to say.

What? There's more? My posture? How important can my body be?

Well, if you play your cards right, it's another way to become invisible.

Mother was right: Stand up straight. Walk tall.

Let's face it. We're more judgmental than we like to think we are. We form instant opinions about people based on how they walk and stand, if they shuffle, strut, swagger, slouch, glide, sashay, or just WALK.

If you see someone dressed in rags, walking with confidence, you assume she's wearing the latest fad. If you see another person in rags, shuffling, you assume something entirely different.

In the movie "Boomerang," Eddie Murphy's body language was a great example: he went from a great confident swagger at the beginning of the film to a shadow of his former self when he lost his confidence. During her performance in "In Search of Intelligent Signs of Life in the Universe," Lily Tomlin changed her posture and became a teenager, a bag lady, a housewife. No imagination required on our part—her posture said it all.

Stand And Deliver

Do you know how you walk? How you stand? Do you know what you're doing with your eyes and your hands? In front of a group, or every day?

Probably not. We don't think much about what our bodies are doing UNTIL—we feel we're in the spotlight. Suddenly we're acutely aware of an inability to control the beast. How to walk across the platform. What to do with those hands. How to sit down.

Solution: Pay attention to what your body is doing when you're not speaking, and you won't have to think about it when you are.

Benefit: Having strong confident posture can encourage you to feel good about whatever you're doing. AND: Feeling good about sharing the information makes you stand stronger, speak stronger, and have more energy. It works both ways.

A few minutes each day, practice one of the things you want to change.

- Correct your posture during the day whenever you think about it.

- Be aware of what your body is doing when you're talking with friends or co-workers.

- Listen to yourself to see if you're saying "and uh," and if you're paying attention to what you're saying, or just talking aimlessly.

- Notice if your walk is positive, toes straight ahead, rib cage lifted out of waist, arms barely swinging.

- Notice whether or not you're looking at people —and *seeing* them.

Work on improving these mannerisms when you're not "on." They'll become part of you and you won't be being somebody else—that will be the real you.

"I Only Have Eyes For You"

When you give a presentation, your eyes may be the most important part of your body. Use them to connect with your listeners. "They need to know you care before they care about what you know." Or look at it this way: They don't care about what you know until they know you care. Looking is a form of caring.

BENT OFFERINGS　By Don Addis

Do you need to look them right in the eye? Yes. Why? Because looking at people's foreheads (or at the

. . . .
To feel more comfortable, look into their eyes.
. . . .

wall just over the last row, or at just one friendly face in the audience) doesn't work.

First, if you're not looking at people, they can tell the difference and so can you. You're less focused, less animated and less energetic because you're not talking to anyone. You lose that personal connection.

Second, if you're not looking at them, how do you know if they're interested, nervous, bored, too hot, tired of sitting, puzzled, angry? You need feedback.

Third, if you're looking at only one person, that person is going to be uncomfortable. And everyone else is free to nap since you're obviously not interested in them.

Bonus: Looking at people actually makes you less nervous. It makes you less nervous because you're not confronting a faceless crowd of dubious intent, you're looking from one familiar face to another, talking to one person at a time, not to hordes.

When you *see* them, they seem familiar because they remind you of people you know. They are, after all, just regular folks.

"There Ain't No Way To Hide Your Lyin' Eyes"

Is eye contact really that important? Go to the movies and watch their eyes—on the screen, that is. If their bodies give one message, voices give another, and the eyes something else, we're confused or we think they should hire another actor. Passionate eyes stay focused, no shifting. Total focus. Terrified eyes do, too. Anxious eyes dart. Confident eyes focus without shifting, but more casually, with less tension.

When Bob saw himself on video tape for the first time in class, he exclaimed, "No wonder I'm losing control of the meetings. I look scared!" He'd had a problem looking at people—eyes all over the place, everywhere except seeing anyone.

Lou made it through the eye contact exercise just fine, looking at each person for the prescribed length of time, except—he admitted he never saw anyone. The secret lies in actually seeing the people you're talking to just as you presumably do during an important conversation. It's not just looking; it's SEEING.

Richard Nixon during the first of the 1960 debates often looked over at John F. Kennedy from the corner of his eye, rather than turning his head and looking directly at him. (Kennedy looked right at Nixon.) Another piece of the losing puzzle.

Slow your eye movement. Let it linger. Keep it in tune with what you're saying by thinking about what you're saying, not about you. Be aware of talking to the person you're looking at.

"The Attack Of The Killer Tomatoes"

If you never look at people—if you never see them—you imagine a pack of werewolves gathering strength for the attack. The longer you avoid looking at them, the more frightening they become.

On the other hand, looking right at them, and seeing them (including before you get started) helps you focus, and transforms it from a horde to a group of individuals.

Pause. Take your time. Look at them. Recognize that you're talking to just one person at a time—not a faceless crowd. You'll feel much calmer. Practice this until you're sure you've got it. It's one of the most important things you can do to get comfortable.

"Take The I (Eye) Train"

You say you lose your train of thought when you look at people. That's usually because you get caught up in what you think the other person is thinking about you—maybe an earlier discussion about the subject, someone who has control over your job, someone you find attractive. Whatever.

It's not what they're thinking that causes the problem. It's what you're thinking. If they're thinking nice things about you and you're sure they're not, guess who's causing the problem?

Solution: Pause, look at someone else, refocus, and go on. Don't ignore that person, just don't go back to

CALVIN AND HOBBES By Bill Watterson

him until you're back on track. Remember, you're talking to individuals, not to personalities. Everyone in that room is important.

The point of eye contact is to connect with your audience.

Like most other things about speaking, what's good for you is good for your audience.

"Raise Your Hand If You're Sure"

You go to a lot of trouble to organize, practice, check the equipment, and then you blow it because you don't sound like you mean what you're saying. We unconsciously respond to how people say a thing to decide if we believe what they say. Inflection before content.

When you're sure of your position, sure of your message, unworried about criticism, and you're focused, your voice sounds confident, convincing and truthful. Worrying about anything (including whether you're going to

GRIN & BEAR IT   **By Wagner**

"You delivered your sermon with passion and authority, but it was my shopping list by mistake."

remember your material), or going on autopilot, sends your voice into strange places giving conflicting messages. Your voice says one thing, your words another.

In an ordinary conversation, when you state a fact, you state it. Period. In a presentation, if your mind is elsewhere, instead of stating that fact, it comes out as a question. We're number one? The project is right on schedule? We're not having any problems?

To avoid sending conflicting signals, think about what you're saying as you say it. Mean it, or don't bother saying it.

It sounds so simple, until we start doing it in class. Stand up and say your name as a fact. No question mark. Just say it. That usually goes pretty well. The trouble comes when you add something to that, and say something in addition to your name. "My name is Jose Jimenez. I'm an astronaut with NASA."

Ninety out of a hundred people will say their names with a rising inflection as though it's a question, when introducing themselves to a group. Can you imagine what that sounds like? Can you see how confusing it is to people if you're saying one thing with your words and another with your voice? Are you feeling the effect here of too much rising inflection with this last set of questions? You're probably introducing yourself as though you're not sure who you are, giving the impression that you also may not know what you're doing.

· ·

Avoid rejection caused by inflection

· ·

This is a hard one. Record yourself telling someone the name of your favorite restaurant. Next, tell your name in that same positive tone (picture a period after it). Third, say your name with that positive tone (period), and then your job title. Play it back and see if any of it sounds uncertain, if any of the parts sound like a question instead of a statement.

We automatically inflect correctly in conversation (when we're participating and not on auto pilot) because we mean what we say. In giving a presentation, we don't do it because instead of participating, instead of meaning what we say, we're too concerned with getting the information right, so we're focused on notes or we go on autopilot.

Be there. Think about what you're saying, not what you're going to say. And practice listening for other people's inflections. Most national newscasters have a good grip on their inflection. Most amateurs don't unless they've let their passion outweigh their self-consciousness.

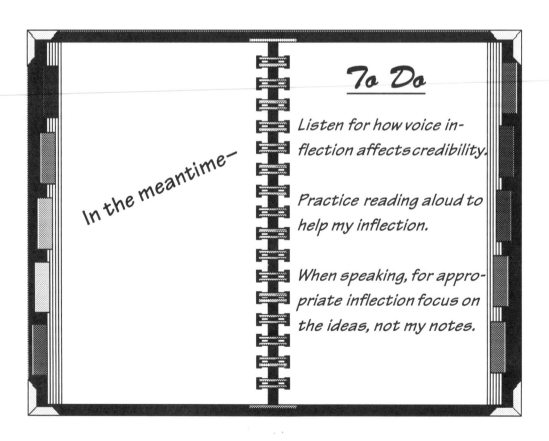

In the meantime—

To Do

Listen for how voice inflection affects credibility.

Practice reading aloud to help my inflection.

When speaking, for appropriate inflection focus on the ideas, not my notes.

11

No, They Can't Take Those Away From Me

"We All Need Somebody To Lean On"

You say you need a lectern. I don't think so. You can't fool the audience just because they can't see all of you. If you're shaking enough for the audience to see it, the lectern won't cover that up. Or the death grip, or the bad posture. It shows.

In the 1988 presidential debates, Walter Mondale could be seen shifting his weight several times before answering each question, and he was standing behind a lectern. In that year's vice-presidential debate, Dan Quayle, affected his posture by standing with his weight on his back foot, his front foot resting on the lectern. Neither candidate looked especially confident, and the lectern didn't hide their posture.

Get out from behind that lectern. It's not your friend. We wait till we're behind one to get a grip—a death grip. If you're a white knuckle speaker, it shows. Grip the lectern, lock your elbows, clamp your jaw, hunch your shoulders. It doesn't show? Right.

Lean on it, rest, play with the texture, shift your weight. It shows.

And you aren't going to have to duck behind it. They aren't going to throw things. Trust me on this.

If you must use a lectern, don't lean on it, grip it, play with it, or abandon your posture and gestures. They'll see all those things and draw unfavorable conclusions.

And if the microphone is attached to the lectern, maybe you can stand beside it, and bend the microphone into place. (Be careful you don't unconsciously drape yourself on the lectern.) Or ask for a separate lavaliere microphone that clips on your collar or lapel.

Better to learn to control your body, face the audience, and connect with them comfortably just in case there is no lectern.

Come out. Make friends. Connect. There's less pressure on you because it's easier to consider yourself "one of the family." Much harder to do behind the lectern.

It can be a convenient place to put your notes (if you're brave enough to use them). Sometimes the microphone is attached to it, and it will hide the spot on your skirt, or the fact that your shoes don't match. (And, to be fair, in some situations you need to project an air of authority or formality that the lectern provides.)

Other than that, try to avoid using one. It keeps you from connecting with your audience physically and psychologically. You're supposed to be convincing them you're one of them. That's harder to do, standing behind a lectern. You seem more remote, and you may feel that way as well.

Even if your notes are on the lectern, you don't have to stand behind it. You can always walk back and look at them if you need to. (More on this in the section on notes.)

Before succumbing to the siren song of the lectern, consider whether it's worth risking separating yourself —mentally and physically—from your audience. You need to connect to collect (make the sale, that is.)

"I Don't Need No Stinkin' Lectern"

What if you're expected to use one? What if they make you use one? What if everyone else is using a lectern?

Go back to the lesson on listening. Get tuned in to the big picture—the IDEA—not your fear and emotions. If the idea (the occasion, the audience, your purpose) says "no lectern" consider your options. Can you move it? Can you stand beside it (bend the mike over to you)?

Can you get out in front? Get down into the crowd? (Be sure you can be seen by everyone.)

Got it? In other words, don't automatically accept a set up or a mind set. It's okay to ask for what you want. Including house lights up, spots down if it will help you connect with your audience and support the message (make the sale).

That's plan A. What if it doesn't work? What if the answer to all those questions is no. Or after quietly considering the possibilities you realize it would be so uncomfortable (mentally or physically) for someone to make the change, and so logistically difficult, it would cancel any possible benefits?

Plan B is to accept it gracefully and consider how best to connect in spite of the lectern. Think of it as a challenge—or that great word opportunity—to prove you can make 8 the hard way. You can connect and make everyone feel included.

Rest arms (not your weight) lightly on the lectern: this way you're free to gesture and nothing gets tense. Lean into the audience, using the lectern as a springboard to connect rather than a barrier for protection.

Be even more conscious of seeing people and connecting with them. Smile (genuinely) at some people before you start. Relax. Take your time to get a feel for who's out there and let them get comfortable with you.

To Note Or Not To Note, That Is The Question

Should you use notes? What? You say you've never even considered talking without notes, that you'd rather bungee jump? Well maybe you should (consider talking without notes, that is). You might be a happier, better communicator.

Carol was surprised at how free she felt when she finally gave up using notes. It took her two years to make the complete break, but she was elated at how much better she connected with her audience and her material. And how much more she enjoyed herself.

Tom tried it in his first talk after being in class. He left something out of his talk, but because of his new found poise, it didn't bother him and he included it at another place and it worked fine.

Tom and Carol both got excellent comments from their audiences.

It's not that using notes is "evil;" it's that they can do more harm than good.

When can you safely use notes? When you don't need them anymore. Otherwise, they occupy too much of your attention.

FRANCIE By Sherrie Shepherd

Using notes can paralyze you because you feel compelled to say what you wrote on them. They also encourage you to leave the information in your notes rather than capturing it in your head. With all that going on there's no way you can connect (and communicate) with the audience.

"You've Gotta Have Heart"

You've gotta have heart, confidence, and experience to connect with an audience while reading text. Colin Powell did it in his address to Howard University—he connected with the ideas he was reading, and with his audience. Ronald Reagan did it. But if you were at that point, you probably wouldn't need this book.

Notes tend to make you look down for the next idea (for the purpose of being smooth) just as you're making your most important point, thereby losing the impact.

And before giving the talk, you're likely to keep reviewing your notes instead of thinking about the ideas you want to communicate. And sometimes (because you're reviewing only on the surface of your brain, trying to remember the words, not ideas), the more you review your notes the more sure you are that you don't know what you're talking about.

Once you arrive and the program begins, don't think about your notes or your presentation. Listen to the other speakers. You'll feel less nervous, and you may pick up some information that will make your talk better.

"Words, Words, Words"

Perhaps you've tried the key word approach to notes, just jotting down a few key words or bullet points. It's a good one and works for a lot of people. My problem with it (before I got over being nervous) was that I would look at those key words and think, "Hm, I'd better have a few more words; I'm not going to remember this."

A few more words would go on the notes. Still not enough. Eventually, I'd have so many words I'd revert to reading whole sections.

If you have that problem, try using pictures, instead of words, for your notes. It's easier to lock onto and interpret a single picture standing in for a whole idea, than to interpret some black marks on a page that require processing.

The walk signal at the intersection is a simple example. Some signals say "Walk," some have an icon of a figure walking. You probably have no trouble reading the word "Walk," but your mind processes the picture faster and with less effort.

The letters of the alphabet look the same from word to word, making it hard to remember exactly which word and which letters you had in mind for this idea. A picture chosen to represent an idea, uniquely selected for the purpose, is much easier to remember.

After organizing your talk, sit back and think about the main ideas you're expressing. See if you can run through it without looking at anything. Think of your speech in chunks, not in detail. What are the main chunks of it? Next, think of the first chunk and what points support it, again, not details, but broad strokes. Continue through each section.

Next, do a brainstorming session with yourself (be off-the-wall here) as to possible visual representations those big chunks bring to mind. Talking about schedules, timetables, importance of meeting deadlines, production goals, delivery needs, could bring to mind a clock, an hour glass, calendar, starting blocks (for a race), a whip, snail, pony express, envelope with stamp, a parent with small child dawdling behind, someone pushing a mule, a jar of molasses, a finish line.

How many more can you come up with? Which ones can you draw easily (not well, just easily). No one else has to see this; it's just to jog your memory. Stick figures are okay. Do you have a clip art library on your computer? Look through those pictures for possibilities.

"Unforgettable"

The abstract concepts are usually the biggest challenge to develop pictures for, but they also may be the very ideas you need the most help remembering. Taking the time to do pictures for them may save your bacon.

These can be totally silly. Often the silly ones are easiest to remember. Since no one else sees them, they don't have to pass a test for appropriateness. Have some fun with this, because whether you actually take the pictures with you as notes, or just take them in your head, at uncomfortable moments (such as losing your place), pause and refocus, and those pictures will pop right back in your head.

Interestingly, when it comes time to decide on visual aids, some of the pictures you choose for notes may (with a little professional help) be appropriate visual aids. After all, if it helps you remember the idea, it will probably have the same effect on your audience.

"Have You Got Cheating On Your Mind?"

When you stop thinking of a presentation as a test, you'll realize that getting help to make it come out right isn't cheating.

For instance, when your boss tells you to present data on your project, it somehow doesn't seem cricket to ask what specifically would be the most helpful information for you to tell her. And it feels like cheating when you look at your notes. It's okay to do both of those things.

Keep in mind the purpose of the talk—to impart information useful to the audience. If asking about the prospective audience during the preparation phase helps do that, that's good. And if, during the talk, you need to check your notes to be sure you continue to be accurate, or on target, that seems good. So forget the furtive little glances.

Who cares if you look at your notes? I'd rather (as an audience member) have you look at them and get it right, than have you jumble it up. Remember that during a pause, your audience thinks about what you just said. It gives them time to catch up. Pauses and looking at your notes are not signs of feeblemindedness. But furtive glances look silly. Stop talking, look at your notes, don't be afraid of the silence, take your time, get what you need and start again.

This works—once you've reached the point where they are a safety net, not a crutch.

In the meantime—

My Goal

To become so
comfortable I won't
need any crutches:
notes, no notes,
lectern, no lectern,
I'm happy.

Try using pictures
for my notes and
see if it works.

MANAGING YOUR WORDS

12

"Put 'Em Together And What 'Ya Got? Bibbity Bobbity Boo"

"This Time We Almost Made The Pieces Fit"

Very early in his remarks at Howard University, General Colin Powell noted that the big challenge when preparing a talk like this "is to figure out how long you are going to talk. . . . If you ask the students, they'll say four minutes. . . . If you ask the parents, they want their money's worth. Two or three hours would be about right."

With any luck, you'll be given a time limit. Consider it a blessing: you're forced to narrow your topic to a manageable size. And even if you think they haven't given you enough time? Look at it as a challenge to see if you can come in 5-10% short of the allotted time.

127

And if they've asked you to talk for longer than 20 minutes, you'd better be pretty entertaining, because that's about it before audiences begin to fade.

Take the time limit seriously. Don't try to cram in more information than there's time for. If you give in to the temptation to add "just a little more," you'll race to get it all in and nobody will absorb *any* of it. It's easy (and not unusual) to think, "If I talk faster, I can say it all."

Keep it short. Usually your audience has other things they could be doing, even if they want to hear what you have to say. Say everything you need to say, but keep to your main point, giving only as much detail as you need for this audience.

When you think it's about right, look at it one more time. Ask yourself, "Could I leave this out?" "Would it still make sense if I left this out?" "Would an example

DILBERT reprinted by permission of United Feature Syndicate, Inc.

make the point better than this explanation?" "Would a graphic explain this more quickly than words?"

"Time, Ticking Away"

You walk into the board room ready to deliver the 30 minutes of slides and detailed information they asked you for, and the chair says: "Got an emergency. Just go over the highlights. I can give you 10 minutes." Ulp!

One participant confessed his experience when a major client did that to him. His competitors (who gave their presentations earlier in the day) all ran over their allotted time, and the "chief" had a plane to catch. Our man panicked and launched into a recitation of the entire presentation at break neck speed. Nobody got any

When I'm organizing—

Memo to me

Keep it as short as possible, remembering how restless I get when a speaker talks too long.

Have a shorter version ready in case they slash my time.

of his information, they surely weren't impressed with his credibility, and he didn't get the account.

You might ask yourself when it happens if you should give a shortened version, or if it would be better to reschedule. Which will serve the audience and your message the best?

It happens. We're always surprised. And we talk ⌐*REAL FAST*⌐. We sweated over preparing. We sweated over the impact on our job. We sweated over the ramifications to the company. We've just sweated on general principles. And we're not going to have all that sweat be for nothing.

If you try to cram 30 minutes of information into 10 minutes, you're wasting your time (and theirs). You certainly won't pause, so they won't have time to assimilate it. And if you don't pause you're out of control, and it shows. So who's going to believe you? I don't think it's putting too fine a point on it to say that the least you have done is waste your time. Worse: You've lost credibility.

The solution: alternate plans. Plan A is the whole presentation. Plan B is a shortened version you prepared first. Plan a short, medium and almost full presentation when you first start preparing. Short, first, with the most important stuff. Build on it and add your next most compelling stuff for a medium presentation. And again for the full thing.

Remember the purpose of a presentation: to reassure the audience they're in good hands. You can be trusted and believed. A calm, poised presentation gives them that reassurance.

"Give Me 5 Minutes More, Only 5 Minutes More"

One effective way to manage your time (and get a better grasp on your material) is to first develop a 3 minute talk. (If I only had 3 minutes, what must I include?)

Continue to build it in increments—10 minutes, 20 minutes—until it's the right length. (The right length is usually a few minutes shorter than you've been allotted.)

Usually, when you organize for a 20 minute talk, you'll end up with 30 minutes, and not know what to cut. (It runs long because of a mistaken notion that more is better, that long means you're being responsible, and that it's important to suffer appropriately.) By then it all looks important and you can't leave anything out. Building from short to long helps avoid that problem.

Benefits: This method also helps when you arrive on the scene and someone says, "Sorry, we can only give you 10 minutes" instead of the 30 you'd been expecting. You've already prepared that one.

· ·

If I had only 3 minutes, what must I tell them?

· ·

And perhaps best of all, by building in blocks of time, you've usually absorbed the structure and the content well enough to speak without notes.

Parts Is Parts

The "parts" to a speech are only to help you stay on track and get to where you want to go.

They're intended to be a key to freedom, not a strait jacket. The usual description: Open, body, close.

An alternate description: Open, bridge, thesis, support, close. A rose by any other name would still be an orderly speech.

- Opening, bridge and thesis = Opening.
- Support = body.
- The close is the close is the close is the close.

The purpose of the parts:

- Opening: get their attention
- Bridge: connect it to them (what's in it for them?)
- Thesis (tell 'em what you're going to tell 'em): tell them where you're headed
- Support (tell 'em): do it
- Close (tell 'em what you told 'em): wrap it up / get them involved in your cause

The opening and bridge together are the hook to capture their attention before making your point.

Organize by choosing your thesis statement first, continuing with support and close. After deciding what you're going to tell 'em (thesis statement), telling 'em (support), and telling 'em what you told 'em (close), you'll be better equipped to decide how to get them to listen —to choose your opening and bridge (how you're going to get them to listen).

"Wasted Days And Wasted Nights"

Most of us belong to the Scarlett O'Hara School of Speech Making: "I'll think about that tomorrow." We get the assignment and spend the next couple of weeks hoping it will go away. When it doesn't, about two days before the presentation we frantically fly into action.

Organizing doesn't have to be a major pain, and you don't have to devote your life to it. The key to success is not so much organizing, as deciding where you want to go. Following these suggestions can save you from all that wasted time.

Within 24 hours of the time you receive your assignment, closet yourself for about 15 minutes and focus. Who is your audience? What are their interests, concerns, demographics. What is your objective? (What do you want them to do or think about when you're

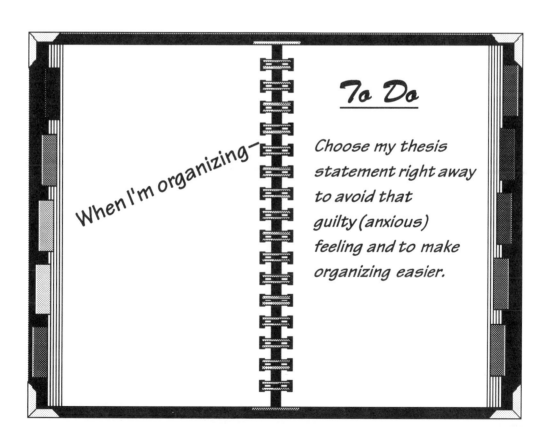

When I'm organizing

To Do

Choose my thesis statement right away to avoid that guilty (anxious) feeling and to make organizing easier.

through?) What is your thesis statement? (Your thesis statement literally says, "I'm going to tell you how . . . , explain why . . . , give you some tips on . . . , tell you three reasons for . . . .")

Those few minutes will pay off. Instead of tossing and turning all night, your presentation will begin to write itself. Knowing where you're headed takes away the uncertainty, and you begin to collect material that otherwise would have meant nothing.

Choose your thesis statement early and you can then use your usual approach—which for most of us means ignoring the assignment until the impending deadline forces us to do something.

Do yourself a favor and try getting your thesis statement as soon as you get the assignment; it's a lifesaver. Deciding specifically where you're going will save you. "The ideas are knocking on your head trying to get in; all you have to do is know what you want, forget about it, and go about your business."

"Are We There Yet, Dad?" (Pity the Poor Audience)

Inside every adult in your audience hides that child asking his parents "are we there yet?" We've grown up enough to keep it to ourselves, but it's still there—"Have we gotten to the point yet?"

Knowing that gives you some clues: Keep it shorter than you had planned, let them know regularly where they are on their trip, and keep them so entertained (focused) they don't think of asking, "Are we there yet?"

Use verbal cues for your sign posts. "By the end of this presentation I'd like to get your buy-in to this project." "To summarize my first point . . . ." "This change will help you . . . ." "Now to wrap this up, the three easiest ways for us to . . . ." Keep yourself and your audience on track.

"Stuck In The Middle With You"

Start organizing by choosing your thesis statement, and the "body" will suggest itself. If your thesis statement is a simple, focused, complete sentence, it will point the way.

In approximately 1 minute from the time he starts speaking to the National Consumers League Conference in May 1995, Edward D. Young III completes his thesis statement and has completely paved the way for the body of his talk (I have not included his brief opening):

"My specific purpose this morning is to share some thoughts with you about how this technology will reach out to the consumer's home as we approach the end of the 20th century.

"I'm going to organize my remarks around three main points. First, . . . I want to talk a bit about the information superhighway, or cyberspace . . . . Second, I'm going to describe some of the services this . . . will make available to consumers. Third and finally, I want to suggest how you . . . can help . . . consumers remain in control . . . ."

This kind of thesis dictates your support — the body of your talk.

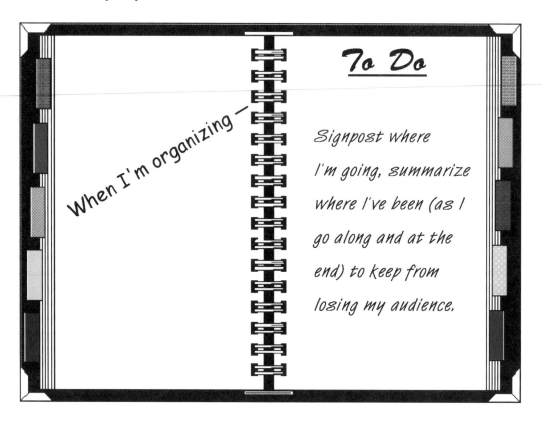

When I'm organizing—

To Do

Signpost where I'm going, summarize where I've been (as I go along and at the end) to keep from losing my audience.

"I Can See Clearly Now"

Mr. Young's thesis led very naturally into Part I, an explanation of the inevitability of the information highway in our lives.

> *"It isn't something you can point to on a map or even on a radar scope and say, 'There it is.' As Gertrude Stein said of Oakland, 'There's no there there.' So it is with the 'Information Superhighway.' It's simply a label or shorthand term to describe the convergence . . . of many different kinds of communications and information networks."*

Which then logically flowed to Part II, services possible to the consumer at home.

> *"You can veg-out if you want to* [on the 500 cable channels], *but you can also avail yourself of information and services that have previously been available only to the privileged few, and in many instances not even to the most wealthy, the most royal, the most powerful."*

He then showed on-screen demonstrations of specific services now available.

And finally to part III, addressing concerns about protection of privacy and confidentiality on the Information Superhighway. A good example of how the support grows naturally from a carefully targeted thesis.

Here are some others: "Today, I'm going to explore with you three ways we can reach our sales goals. We can reach them first by identifying how our recent upgrades specifically relate to that customer's applications; second, by tailoring our presentation more specifically to that customer; and, third, by using more creative visuals."

And:

"I'm going to tell you how increasing our training budget can help us reach our sales goals. My reasons are based on the three main reasons our sales force gives for not making those goals. First, we're hearing a lot of complaints from the field that they're expected to answer questions they know nothing about. Second, morale is slipping because we haven't given them the tools to deal with customer's questions and concerns. And third, they're missing sales because their product knowledge and presentation skills look bad compared to the competition's."

Don't give them too much. Don't try to give them every reason you can think of. Choose the reasons you believe will be most convincing to that particular audience. Weed out the others. Put the extras in a file someplace for another presentation to a different audience.

If you give them too much information, you're wasting your time. They may be polite, but they won't remember it and you won't make the sale.

"I Can Go On No Longer"

Great! Quit while you're ahead. No matter how interested in your subject they are, they've got lives. Less is more. Make your point, deliver your message, and stop.

If the body isn't clear, if you don't make your point, if you haven't suffered enough, you may continue talking, hoping to make up with quantity what you lack in quality.

Sir Winston Churchill said, "Say what you have to say, and when you come to the end of a grammatical sentence, sit down."

"Signed, Sealed, Delivered"

Go for broke on the close. It's your last chance to reach them. And your last chance to make the sale. Remember you're always selling—an idea, a product, your credibility.

General Powell's last words at Howard University's commencement: "Always let your dreams be your only limitation. Now and forever."

Elizabeth Glaser at the Democratic convention: "We need to hope our dreams can come true. I challenge you to help because all our lives depend on it. Not just mine."

Boris Yeltsin eulogizing victims of the military-KGB putsch in August 1991: "It was a difficult loss, and the

• •

"Always let your dreams be your only limitation. Now and forever."

• •

memory of it will be with us forever. For that reason, our heroes, sleep peacefully and let the earth be soft for you."

Edward D. Young III to the National Consumers League Conference:

> *"The real argument in favor of the information superhighway, to my way of thinking, is not so much the economic benefits it brings, but the improvement in the quality of life it will offer.* [An implied summary with benefit.]

> *"Please take a fresh look at the facts. Please take time to carefully assess your position on the issue. Please consider carefully the facts you have learned and will learn during the course of this conference.* [Tells them what to do.]

> *"And then do your best job of being an advocate for the consumers you represent. If you*

do that, we know the consumer and our coun-try will be well served." [What to do and a ben-efit.]

A socko finish leaves them thinking it must have been good, and they ought to accept whatever you've said.

A limp finish weakens everything that came before, leaving everyone wondering if you're through.

Hit the home run. POW! Smack it into the stands. Feel the thrill of seeing it fly over the fence. And then sit down. No "thank you," no uncertainty. (Saying "thank you" brings them back to thinking about you instead of leaving them with your message.)

"Bring In The Clowns"

Once you "Tell 'em what you're going to tell 'em," (thesis statement), "Tell 'em," (support) and "Tell 'em what you told 'em," (close), you've got a nice compact, cohesive presentation. But will anybody want to listen?

Aren't there a few loose ends in your life that keep you from focusing on the speaker (phone calls, appoint-ments, car repairs)? Your audience doesn't usually ar-rive eagerly anticipating your presentation. Even if they're interested in your subject, their thought is scat-tered, thinking about the previous speaker, a crisis in the department, a conversation with the person next to them.

You risk having the audience miss your point by starting with the thesis statement because they're not listening yet. You don't have their attention.

"From 0 To 60 In 60 Seconds"

Go for it. When you open your talk, jump right in —not into the meat of your topic, but with bold words and committed voice. This is no place for being tenta-tive. To make this easy for you: Choose words and an idea you can commit to, words that are easy to say, and short sentences.

While the O. J. Simpson trial was in progress, a speaker in class started boldly with "O. J. is innocent and I know who did it." She delivered it boldly, and then paused long enough for it to sink in. Oh, yes. She had everyone's attention. Granted the subject was an automatic conversation starter, not all openings on the same subject would have been that powerful.

On a business topic, a speaker in another class opened with "I'm going to give you a headache. And then

"You can always count on ol' J.B. for a snappy intro!"

I'll give you an aspirin." Short. Direct. Creative. Visual. Attention getting. Pretty easy for the speaker to remember, too—a real plus for helping you get started.

Openings that feel like the the middle of a conversation get quick attention, as do starters such as, "Imagine this . . . ," "Suppose . . . ." or "What if . . . ?"

If you choose an opening that appeals to you, you'll start stronger and more confidently.

"Once Upon A Time . . . ."

An address by Sir Shridath Ramphal to the 22nd Congress of World Federalists Movement in San Francisco, started with

> *"A long time ago now, it must have been in the late 1960s, I received from you . . . a communication that I cherished greatly then— and still do. I was a young Foreign Minister. . . ."*

This combines a "once upon a time" approach, with a personal experience, and a connection to that particular audience.

Yes. Start organizing by choosing your thesis statement. (You're more likely to accomplish your purpose if you start by deciding what that purpose is.) But don't *deliver* the thesis until they're with you.

If you open with your thesis statement, you may be the only one who hears it. That's where your opening comes in. Say something interesting—lead off with some part of the subject that the audience is sure to care about. (And to make it easier for you to get started, make sure it's something you care about.)

For an in-house presentation, that start could be recent survey results on your product versus your competitor's. Or a customer's testimonial (or complaint). Or something that happened in your department recently that illustrates the point. Be a little more creative than starting with, "Here's the data."

Maybe something you've used in the support would be a good lead in. Maybe one of those things you decided to leave out of the support would work. Maybe something you closed with would bear repeating and you could start and end with it.

Questions, examples, quotations, stories, startling statements, current news, something particularly relevant to this audience or this occasion, a familiar advertising slogan—think!

You'll see ideas to adapt everywhere when you start looking. In an airline magazine: "As the manager of the Manhattan Fund, I love growth stocks. But I don't think love should be blind." A bookstore ad: "Tip O'Neill is to

In the meantime—

Memo to me

Start collecting interesting phrases, humorous happenings, ad slogans, t-shirt sayings, etc.
Business presentations should be interesting.

the right of Barry Goldwater." A billboard for a gymnasium: "You can rest when you're dead."

Have You Heard The One About . . . ?

Unless you're great with humor, don't pressure yourself to start with a joke. If it bombs, you die (or wish you had).

Would the Gettysburg address, or Martin Luther King Jr.'s "I Have a Dream" speech, have been better if they'd started with jokes?

You've all heard rules for joke-telling that recommend against telling off-color, religious, or racial jokes. Pay attention to those rules. You may also want to consider these criteria: You can tell a joke if 1) You know the joke so well you can't blow the punch line; 2) It relates to your topic (rather than just to get a laugh); and 3) It won't bother you if no one laughs.

CROCK   By Bill Rechin and Don Wilder

Reprinted with special permission of North America Syndicate

Number 3 is easier to deal with if you've observed number 2. Because it relates to your subject, you can easily make your point and move on—because there was a point. Also, remember that people may get the point, and even have thought it was funny, without actually laughing out loud.

There are lots of other ways to start that you probably will feel more comfortable with. And if it's humor you want, something humorous that happened in the office or with a customer can be a lot easier to tell, and removes the pressure of thinking you have to tell a joke well, remember the punch line, and worry about anyone laughing.

"The Knee Bone's Connected To The Thigh Bone"

Everything's got to connect. The topic has to connect to the audience, the opening has to connect to the thesis, every section has to connect with the ones on either side. Giving a speech is a matter of connecting islands.

When you take a good look at your opening, you may find you already have the bridge; you've hooked the audience, and you've also directly related it to their interests.

Maybe you've got the perfect opening, but if there's a gap between it and your thesis you need a bridge, a way to connect the two thoughts.

Or, you've got a great opening, a real attention getter, but the audience doesn't feel involved; you need a bridge—a way to connect what you've said (and what's coming), to your audience.

The bridge isn't a contrivance, form without function; it's a connector.

In Sir Shridath Ramphal's address, he bridged to his audience immediately by referring to a communication he had received from that particular audience.

"Like A Bridge Over Troubled Waters"

The bridge comes quite early in your speech, somewhere in the first few sentences. Without a good connection you can further separate yourself from an unwilling audience. But used effectively, it can help persuade an audience that you're okay, and it's safe to listen to your message.

Governor Mario Cuomo did it implicitly in his speech to the 1988 Democratic Convention when he used the widespread relief created by the return of troops from the Persian Gulf War, as a bridge to his audience —a bonding agent.

He connected them to his message and to himself; he showed that they had something in common. That's an important element in persuasion, and you're almost always persuading (selling).

If you've started with the most recent survey information comparing your product to your competitor's product, that may be enough to make them want to hear more.

Perhaps, though, you could make it even more relevant by saying something that links that information to your audience's particular concern. How does this information directly affect the work they are doing?

Prime Minister Ingvar Carlsson to the council on Foreign Relations at the United Nations after one sentence acknowledging the 50th anniversary occasion, bridges directly ("a concern I am sure many of you share with me,") and indirectly ("I . . . hope . . . might rouse the 185 shareholders") with his audience.

> *"Sadly, there is more concern than celebration in this week's commemoration of the UN's anniversary — a concern I am sure many of you share with me. . . .*
>
> *"Forty percent of this year's regular budget remains unpaid. If the UN were an American corporation we would be talking about Chapter 11 or worse.*
>
> *"Nevertheless, I have not given up hope that the UN's current situation might rouse the 185 shareholders into making a new beginning . . . ."*

Note, too, his analogy of an American corporation and Chapter 11, a good rhetorical device he continues with reference to the 185 shareholders.

"Without You I Have Nothing At All"

Throughout your speech, you're trying to get them personally involved. You want them to feel you're talking specifically to them, and that they need to respond. You need to establish that (get them involved) right from the beginning. Get the "good stuff" going right away.

The more it's about them, the less it's about you—and you're invisible. Keep them thinking about themselves all the way through. And start doing it early.

When I'm organizing—

To Do

Connect everything I say to the audience. What do they care about this? How will it affect their work? What's in it for them?

That's the purpose of setting up a special category of your organizing, called the bridge. Be sure you get them to feel your topic is relevant to them. Give them benefits to them, describe problems that affect them. People respond more positively, and more quickly if they feel involved.

You're making it clear that it's not about you, and letting them know they're the whole reason for this occasion.

A sign in a store being remodeled: "Pardon our dust while we're improving your store."

"You Take The High Road And I'll Take The Low Road"

If you are quite clear on what you want to say, and what you want the audience to do, you'll probably succeed.

If you're having trouble comfortably arranging your material, check your thesis; you may not be specific enough about what you want to do. Look at it again, and see if you've made your destination obvious.

You may also need to choose an organizational pattern for presenting the information logically.

Does it make sense to compare or contrast your findings, your information, your suggestions, with a previous point in the research or sales, or another company?

Would it be better presented chronologically, or in sequence of what must be done, or of what has happened up to this point?

Do you have several equivalent topics that all need to be covered? Put them in 2, 3, 1 order, or 1, 3, 2 order based on the fact that people tend to remember best the first and last things said. Something you really want them to remember may be said first and then repeated at the end.

"One, Two, Three, That's How Easy It's Gonna Be"

If you think in outlines, use one to help you organize. Most people wince at the thought, hence the invention of clusters, mind-mapping and other methods for grouping your thoughts in search of an orderly presentation.

You don't need to outline; you do need to make sure your points are evenly weighted—which is the basic principle of an outline.

After deciding on your thesis statement, jot down all the main support points (reasons) you can think of that back up your thesis. Pick out the ones that very naturally and clearly lead from it. (Can you make a sentence out of your thesis and support?)

"We need to spend more money on training because we're wasting all the money we spent on product development." (An attention grabber—we're wasting money—doesn't hurt in your thesis. You want to keep their attention throughout.)

Reasons:

- We don't know the advantages (features?) of that product

- We're not clear on how to use it

- We're not clear on how to tell other people about it

- We're fumbling in front of the customer

- We don't know the answers to their questions

- We're taking too much time with the sales calls

Some of these explain the others—they support the support. (They could be Capital A or B under Roman numeral I or II, if you like outlines). Some of them you may not want to use at all.

Choose those most likely to win your audience.

"From Freeways To Sports (Transitions)"

You can change direction almost radically so long as you telegraph the change to your audience and take them with you. Lead them; don't yank.

Transitions can be as simple as having a substantial pause, or saying, "Now," or "First off," "In the other direction," "Let's move to another application," "And yet," or "But think about this."

Listen to a news anchor team. Often their transition consists of using the other anchor's name to move to a totally unrelated story.

· ·

Transition: Lead your audience from point to point

· ·

The title of this section is an example from a news broadcast. That was the transition: "From freeways to sports," and off they went with all of us obediently following in the new direction.

When you go, take us along. Blow in our ears and we'll follow you anywhere.

"Baubles, Bangles, Bright Shiny Beads"

Another way to help you get your audience to follow you anywhere is to incorporate the "Rule of Three" in your presentations.

There's something about using three points, repeating a sound three times or repeating a word or an idea three times that makes your message easier to remember.

"Baubles, bangles, bright shiny beads" is much catchier than "emeralds, diamonds and pearls." This particular example of the rule also repeats the "B" sound three times—a double punch.

Another effective use of the rule is to repeat the same word or phrase. Colin Powell did this very effectively in a speech kicking off his Volunteer America campaign: "We cannot fail if . . . ." "We cannot fail if . . . ." "We cannot fail if . . . ."

Mario Cuomo applied the "Threes" another way in supporting the nomination of Bill Clinton at the 1992 National Democratic Convention: "Smart enough to know, strong enough to do, sure enough to lead."

Be smart, strong and sure. Use the Rule of Three.

"Are You Ready?"

What about those times when you don't get to prepare? Questions in a meeting. Someone unexpectedly asking you to say a few words at the ground breaking ceremony. Your boss asking for a quick review of your department when you meet on the elevator

You'd like to yell "I'm not ready." But it's usually not an option. In some cases, however, you should consider one of the following: Saying no, suggesting someone else, talking on another subject that you do feel prepared to say a few words on, or of offering to bring the requested information in later. (Choosing those options should be in response to your listening—getting tuned into the big picture instead of your anxiety.)

Whatever you say, whether it's "no," or "I'll get back to you," or you answer the question, say it confidently. Forget apology, uncertainty or defensiveness.

"Give Me Hope, Help Me Cope"

Use your ability to pause and listen for the appropriate response to the request, take a moment to determine your direction, and say it briefly and with conviction.

During the pause use the PREP formula to help you focus. Point, Reason, Example, Point, or use a slightly

REAL LIFE ADVENTURES By Gary Wise and Lance Aldrich

It's tough to gather your thoughts when
you have no idea where they are.

more effective variation, the PERP formula—giving your
example before the reason.

Ask yourself what the POINT you want to make to
this audience is or what your point of view is as it relates to this audience. This is equivalent to your thesis
statement. Reduce your point to its simplest form, so
you can say it without getting lost in the words.

Give an EXAMPLE that illustrates your point,
something that involves the product, person or idea in
a story, an experience.

The example will vividly speak to your REASON,
which you need now only to state briefly, before repeating your POINT.

The example and reason are your support, restat-
ing your point is the close. You've used the structure of
an organized speech without the Opening and Bridge
which are inherent in an impromptu. The opening and

an organized speech without the Opening and Bridge which are inherent in an impromptu. The opening and bridge are used to get the audience's attention. In an impromptu, the questioner provides the attention getter by asking the question.

Once again, we have the basic structure: "Tell 'em what you're going to tell 'em; tell 'em; tell 'em what you told 'em."

Pause. Don't feel personal. Focus on who your audience is and the appropriate point to make. Say it with confidence and good eye contact. Be brief. Stop.

If you find yourself being surprised often by people asking you to say a few words at unctions, stop being surprised and plan ahead. Think of one or two good all purpose mottos, or stories, that you can use on any occasion. If you're called on unexpectedly, tailor a point to fit that particular occasion.

"It's A Lover's Question"

A good example of an impromptu speech is a question and answer session. Use the same approach here as with everything else we've talked about. Pause and breathe. As a matter of fact, use all four of the major points in this book: Pause, Breathe, Focus and Listen. One class came up with a mnemonic device for remem-

. . . .
Pause, Breathe, Focus, Listen
. . . .

bering PBFL: Peanut Butter For Lunch. Whatever it takes for you to remember, do it.

things personally, to respect your audience and give them the benefit of the doubt, and to let them know you care.

And just to make sure no one leaves with the wrong idea about your message, be sure you repeat your main point at the end of the questions. Yes, that means you will close twice. Once before you ask for any questions. And again afterwards.

• •
At the end of the Q&A:
Repeat your main point.
Close twice .
• •

"Friendly Persuasion"

Most audiences are friendly. However, not all will share your point of view. Or they may oppose your cause, which makes them seem (perhaps quite convincingly) unfriendly.

Barbara Bush, as First Lady in early 1990, was entangled in controversy for being the speaker for Wellesley College's graduation. She wasn't the first choice, and many graduating seniors felt she wasn't a proper role model because she hadn't had a career. There was no lack of publicity on the subject and no lack of emotion.

Her speech throughout was well designed to win the audience. Two examples of her persuasive approach:

1) Less than two minutes into her speech she said, "Now I know your first choice today was Alice Walker—guess how I know." (Of course, it had been thoroughly covered in the press.) And proceeded to weave appropriate comments about Alice Walker, the graduates, and her message in one short paragraph.

2) Just as her speech was closing, she used a piece of humor quite connected to the controversy. "Who knows: somewhere out in this audience may even be someone who will one day follow in my footsteps and preside over the White House as the President's spouse. (Pause) And I wish him well."

Her attitude throughout was confident and friendly. Her message couched in terms and experiences her audience could relax, relate, and listen to.

Organize your message rationally and reasonably. Speak to their interests. Answer their objections.

. . . .
Look at a presentation from your audience's point of view.
. . . .

Persuading someone to listen to your point of view requires you to acknowledge theirs; if you know they have reservations about your subject or your point of view, bring it out in the open, and deal with it.

Mr. Young:

> *"First of all, let me acknowledge that not everyone is in love with the idea of the information superhighway or the services it will bring. For example, John Dvorak, a personal computer columnist, I'm told, calls it the 'information cow path,' and 'a crock of bull cheese.' Humorist Art Buchwald says he is recommending a five-day jail sentence for anyone who uses the term."*

He then impersonally mentions several objections people have, and briefly gives reasonable food for thought while answering the objections. And after listing some benefits, gives a visual presentation of some of the exciting information and research possibilities currently available on the Internet.

For maximum results, always look at a presentation from your audience's point of view. And realize there's some element of persuasion in every presentation.

"What We Have Here Is A Failure To Communicate."

President Reagan was nicknamed "The Great Communicator" because he made it easy for people to listen to him. If your audience doesn't listen, to quote Strother Martin in "Cool Hand Luke," "What we have here is a failure to communicate."

What are some of the reasons Reagan was able to get people to listen? According to University of Pittsburgh Professor Ted Windt, "The genius of his communication was to take a complex situation and make it simple—not simplistic but simple."

He used everyday words, and made us feel he was talking to us. For example, in 1981 Reagan outlined four problems of government that had caused "the worst economic mess since the Great Depression."

He didn't get defensive, or take things personally, hence the appellation, "the Teflon President." When the barbs appeared, he grinned, shrugged, and made it a non-issue, such as his "There you go again" response.

"You Light Up My Life"

Other candidates since Reagan have shown earmarks of his style. Ross Perot captured major attention with his homespun analogies on big government problems.

Senator Phil Gramm on balancing the budget: "Then we'll [Congress] have to cut up at least one of our credit cards."

Gramm again, during a campaign speech for the Republican presidential nomination: "You know I earned a Ph.D. in economics after failing 3rd, 7th, and 9th grades." A graceful way of working in credentials without sounding self-important.

Steve Forbes, running for the Republican presidential nomination, campaigning for radical tax reform, used vivid imagery to make his point about the current tax code: "The only way to change it is to get rid of it. The only thing to do with the monster is to scrap it, kill it, drive a stake through its heart and bury it." He got a lot of media attention with that line.

Big businesses strive to give the effect of being reachable, of being in touch with regular people. The wine company that gave us two folksy old timers on the porch (one silent, one chatting) Home Savings creating a warm and fuzzy image of the banking industry by taking us back to the old days of the '50s, while also staying up-to-date using the slogan: "Banking the way it used to be (except for the computers and stuff)."

Simple, not simplistic. Human connections.

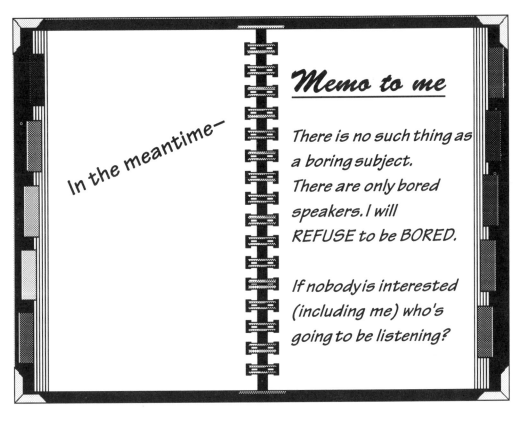

In the meantime—

Memo to me

There is no such thing as a boring subject. There are only bored speakers. I will REFUSE to be BORED.

If nobody is interested (including me) who's going to be listening?

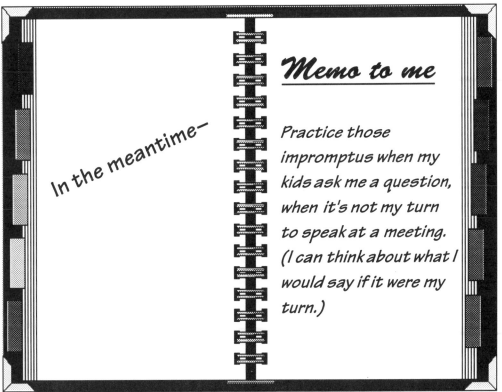

In the meantime—

Memo to me

Practice those impromptus when my kids ask me a question, when it's not my turn to speak at a meeting. (I can think about what I would say if it were my turn.)

13

"Seeing Is Believing"

I'm From Missouri. Show Me.

Or, when is a visual aid not a visual aid? When it's designed as the speaker's notes.

Visual aids can paralyze your mind as efficiently as notes. If you don't have the right attitude, you're more involved with them than you are with communicating. Both visual aids and notes are okay used as safety nets, treacherous when used as crutches. Refer to section on notes to wean yourself from needing them.

Visual aids designed to keep *you* on track, are boring; while designing them, you're focused on saving yourself, not on helping your audience. So you have bullets and words, words and bullets.

Shift gears. Design them to help your audience understand, and they'll work as your notes, too. (It's a miracle.) Your visuals will be more creative and memorable, too.

BEETLE BAILEY   By Mort Walker

Reprinted with special permission of King Features Syndicate

Visuals? No Problem. We've Got Some Nifty Software.

Confucius and every major ad agency in the world can't be wrong. We respond to visual cues. So why the boring slides? PowerPoint, Presentations, Keynote: The

• • • • • • • • • • • • • • • • • • • •

A list of words is not a visual

• • • • • • • • • • • • • • • • • • • •

good news is they help you organize a professional slide presentation more quickly and with less effort.

The bad news is you can still be boring. Slick, but boring. You can still use too many words, avoid interesting graphics, and not use enough white space. Charts are better than words. Pictures, icons and clip art often communicate better than charts.

Look around you. Take off your corporate blinders and notice how visual the world is. It doesn't have to be cute or cutesy to be visual.

Recently a participant reported having seen a presentation a year earlier where the speaker's visuals were simple icons and pictures. At the time, he wondered about it: His company didn't use that kind of visual. However, a year later, he still remembered the information given. Business has something to do with being practical. If people remember the information, you must be doing something right, and that should qualify as businesslike.

Studies show that when presenters use visuals, the audience learns and remembers more and understands

BENT OFFERINGS   By Don Addis

complex subjects more quickly with less explanation needed.

Let's Get Visual

After laying a solid groundwork for his "information superhighway" speech, and giving several benefits of the highway, Edward Young involved the audience with, "But instead of just talking about the services that will be available to you, let me show you. We've brought a sampling of the types of services we believe will be delivered in the near future by Bell Atlantic."

He also acknowledged the dangers inherent in visuals: "You've got to admit that this is kind of gutsy. We realize we're offering strong temptation to the gremlins who make Murphy's Law work so well, but we figured they were too worn out after the super show they've been

DILBERT reprinted by permission of United Feature Syndicate, Inc.

putting on over at the new Denver Airport to bedevil us. So we decided to risk it. Let's see if its going to work."

Words and numbers (even though you can see them) are not what people mean when they say, "Use visuals." At least not people who know what they're talking about. Using visuals means using something graphic or pictorial that can be quickly grasped without spending much time reading or studying it, and can be easily remembered. If using pictures for your notes helps you re-

"DO THIS"

"DON'T DO THIS!"

member what you want to say, maybe they'll do the same thing for your audience.

If your boss forces you to use lots of numbers, lots of words, do. But do it unwillingly. Don't do it because it's the easy way out, easier than thinking of ways you could express the idea succinctly, more simply and visually. You might even throw in something visual once in a while. Not enough to draw fire, just a trial balloon.

In your presentation one or two people actually do want all that detail. You can still give them the overview, and use something creative and visual to show that big picture. (We're up, we're down, it works this way) before giving the details. Handouts are visuals, too, and may be the most effective way to transfer the details to those who want them.

Talk to your audience focusing on what you're saying to them, not on the visual that's on the screen, or on the one you're about to put up. Visual aids can separate you from your audience as easily and quickly as notes can.

Move toward including more pictures in your visuals (as well as more word pictures in your talk). Light up their **DON'T HIDE BEHIND GRAPHICS** lives, and yours.

"I Can See It In Your Eyes"

Most of the detail delivered in presentations is inappropriate. It should be in handouts.

Presentations are to reassure the audience they've hired the right person or they're about to. In other words, you need to look and sound credible so they can relax. Even the hardest of heads make decisions based on gut instinct—then justify it with the facts, a phenomenon Aristotle noted.

If they're confident about you, and your big picture view is solid, you've fulfilled your major purpose.

If the purpose is to deliver detailed information, write it. It's more efficient and accurate; hand it to them to read it at their convenience. They can reread anything they missed. They can check the facts.

DILBERT reprinted by permission of United Features Syndicate, Inc.

If the purpose is to sell an idea, JUST SAY IT. A *Wall Street Journal* article commended giving a 2-hour team presentation without any notes or any visual aids, the only exception to the no-note rule being when a question came up that could best be clarified with a visual.

"Hello Dolly"

Introducing a speaker is a mini-speech, and should be structured as such. And, it's even easier not to focus on yourself. You're a matchmaker. You're joining the audience and the speaker, helping them feel comfortable with each other so the speaker feels the audience is receptive, and the audience anticipates hearing the speaker what the speaker has to say. If you structure it right, it's even easier to realize it's not about you.

Have an interesting opening, just as you would with a speech, not the same old "Our speaker today . . . ." I once started an introduction with "Will Rogers used to say, 'All I know is what I read in the papers.' Well, all I know is what I read in the papers these days isn't that good." And proceeded to link the speaker's approach to today's news with his topic and his credentials.

Ask yourself: Why do they care about the speech or speaker? Why should they listen? "Why this speaker, on this subject, to this audience?"

Avoid a laundry list of qualifications unless the speaker will be insulted if you leave something out, and if the speaker can affect your life. Choose the most convincing parts of the biography for this audience. You're letting the audience know this speaker is someone worth listening to. It's not your job to lull them into a stupor before the speaker arrives on the spot.

BEETLE BAILEY   By Mort Walker

Reprinted with special permission of King Features Syndicate

Here are a couple places to be careful in an introduction: As you get near the end, you begin to congratulate yourself for making it through. Just that momentary split focus makes you think you've forgotten the speaker's name. You haven't. You've just lost focus. Stop and get it back. You've practiced the speaker's name a dozen times. Take your time to refocus, and you'll have it.

The other place is also at the end. Again, the euphoria of getting to the end making you lose focus causes you to turn to the speaker as you say the name. Look at the audience as you're saying it, not at the speaker.

Remember, the purpose of introducing a speaker is to help the speaker and audience feel comfortable with each other.

VISUAL AIDS SONG

Oh the pain of a presentation
Visual aids bring on trepidation
How many slides and how many foils?
What will I get for all my toils?
Dreams of graphs and charts make me wonder
How many chances I have to make a blunder.

No class, no poise, don't know what you're doin'
Messin' up this speech could lead to your ruin
Drop the slides and stumble on the cord
Avoid the group and look at the board
Where's the pen, what's happened to the flip chart?
I'm blowing my chances from the very start.

Look at the audience for reassurance
They're looking back waiting for a reoccurrence
of the blown out bulb and the dried out pen
The backward slides that you may do again.
Here's your chance to get the promotion
See if you can do it with lots less commotion.

Write big, write bold, use some color,
Pictures and graphs hook; words are much duller
Point at the aid with the closest hand
Near to the screen is where you should stand
Check its placement, affirm all can see
What you're showing and ask frequently.

Keep aid covered both before and after,
A blank white screen can be a distracter.
Keep the lights on and angle the screen
Have extra cords to reach the machine
Keep slides simple, don't use too many
It might be better not to use any.

Don't block the screen, don't play with the pointer
If you blow it, pause and reconnoiter.
You're in charge of the situation
Be in charge, control the presentation
Be calm, stay calm, you're in charge
Then the blunders won't loom that large
Practice, practice, practice, practice.

Ned's Rules for Good Conference Presentations
Organizing

✓   People listening to a dozen talks in a morning are not going to remember more than one or two things you said. You can choose what those one or two things are, or you can abdicate.

✓   Decide in advance what ONE thing you have really come to say, and structure your talk around it.

✓   A list is a bad talk. "All about my experiment, my program, etc." is a bad talk.

✓   Practice your talk with a clock. "I think I've got about enough" does not calibrate a presentation. Running overtime is discourteous to everyone, and your conclusion gets lost.

✓   A good talk has a beginning, a middle, and an end. It tells a story.

Source: Edward J. Stone, Ph.D., Research Physicist, Naval Research Laboratory, Washington, D. C.

Ned's Rules for
Good Conference Presentations

Visuals

✓ Nobody can speak effectively to more than one visual per minute. A complex visual requires 3 or 4 minutes.

✓ On each visual there is ONE important point for you to convey to your listener. Know what it is, and make it. A list is a bad visual.

✓ An icon, cartoon, pictograph or picture communicates much faster, and more memorably than its equivalent in words. A color photo or short video will add interest to your explanation of the problem, what you are doing, or your results.

[Caution: Cartoons on screen must be simple, easy to read, and easily grasped by all.]

Ned's Rules for
Good Conference Presentations
Elements of a Good
20-minute Technical Presentation

✓   Title and Authors (1 visual). Minimal narrative. [Could be on screen as audience arrives.]

✓   Introduction. (1 or 2 visuals) What is the subject area of your talk? What is the general state of knowledge in this area?

✓   Motivation. (1 or 2 visuals) What is the problem you are trying to solve? What good is it? Why should anyone care?

✓   Approach. (1 or 2 visuals) What are YOU DOING, and why is that different or better?

✓   The point. (1 visual) What did you learn, specifically? If you cannot answer this question in one sentence of 25 words or less, you don't know what you came to say.

✓   Results. (1-3 visuals) What small subset of your data proves your point?

✓   Conclusion. (1 visual) What does this mean for your work, other work, the future?

[Caution: If you use a visual at the conclusion, turn it off before making your final remarks to the audience.]

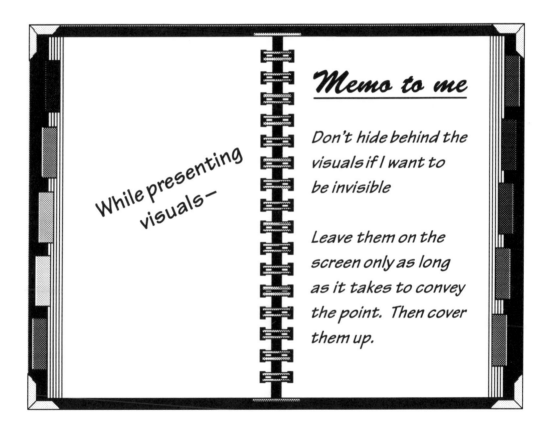

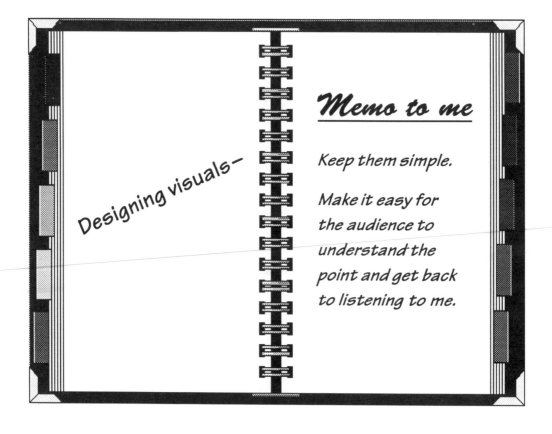

Designing visuals—

Memo to me

Keep them simple.

Make it easy for
the audience to
understand the
point and get back
to listening to me.

SECTION FOUR

MANAGING YOUR SUCCESS

"YOU'VE GOT THE POWER
TO TURN ON THE LIGHT"

14

"Takin' It To The Streets"

"Take A Look At You Now"

This all sounds good, but does it work? And can *I* do it?

Almost everyone faces lingering doubts and fears as they set out to practice the principles in this book.

First, relax. If these principles seem logical to you, if you understand them intellectually, you can apply them successfully.

But that lightning-flash of realization when everything falls into place might not happen while you're giving a presentation. It might occur when you make that hole-in-one, or when you hit that elusive high note, or when you truly connect in a conversation—suddenly you realize you're focused on an idea and not on yourself.

You can speed up the process by being aware daily that you're not the center of anyone else's world. Do you care if someone else's shoes need polishing, or if someone breaks a jar in the market? Probably only if they are part of your life in some way.

Recognize that others are too preoccupied with their own lives to care that much about yours, that's when speaking will become just another (natural) part of your life. You'll begin to discover your mastery a bit at a time.

. . . .

Getting over yourself is like learning to ride a bike— once you learn . . .

. . . .

If you feel awkward your first few times out, remember that everything you've ever learned has followed the four stages in Abraham Mazlow's theory of learning: unconscious incompetency (Ignorance is bliss); conscious incompetency (Oops, I don't know how to do this); conscious competency (I can do this okay if I really pay attention); and unconscious competency (What was the big deal?).

Do you remember learning how to ride a bike? At first, bikes meant nothing to you. Next, you noticed that other kids were riding bikes and you didn't know how. Then, when you tried it, remember feeling that if your Dad let go of the bike you'd fall? And then, when he did let go, how much work it was to stay balanced? Finally one day, you just took off.

First you learn it, then you forget you learned it and just do it because it's yours.

"Let's Give Them Something to Talk About"

Some people came to our seminars feeling like basket cases, hoping only to learn some survival techniques. Here's what some of them had to say about life after class:

Lisa, market research manager who had been panicky about presentations: "The audience loved the presentation, and I realized I forgot to think about the audience's reaction while I was talking. People came up to congratulate me after the talk, and the person in charge told my boss what an outstanding job I had done on the project and the presentation. I received a commendation letter and have been put up for an award!"

• •

"I'm still getting great comments about my speech . . . ."

• •

Lynda, strategic planning advisor: "I'm still getting great comments about my speech at management conference and that was over a month ago. The surprised looks and congratulatory comments started the moment I got off the platform and haven't stopped since. I can't believe it."

David, director of compensation and organization development: "After I presented the plan to the vice-president of compensation for corporate, he said, 'No one can speak to this with the passion and enthusiasm you have. You present it to the next level (President, COO and senior VP'S). They were so excited about the plan, they approved it on the spot. They also complimented me on my presentation, insisting they wanted the top guy in the whole organization to see it. So I presented it to our Chairman and CEO, too. I was floating. I got two voice mails on my outstanding presentation, with comments like, 'You really looked good!'"

Dan, supervisor: "Shortly after taking your class, I made a presentation to management, and felt better than I ever had. It was much easier this time. It must have been successful, too, because I heard later that someone asked, 'Did Dan take a class, or something?' "

James, vice-president, assistant controller: "I recently gave a one-hour presentation to executives of all our corporate entities. It really went great. For that hour I completely forgot about how I was performing. As soon as I finished, my boss complimented me on a good job.

· ·

"Someone else told me my presentation was the best they've seen from me . . . ."

· ·

He followed up the next day with a phone call reiterating his complimentary remarks. He indicated that I looked very calm and took a difficult subject and made it very interesting. Someone else told me my presentation was the best they've seen from me, and also remarked that I took a very 'tough, dull' subject and made it interesting."

Bruce, financial account executive: "The best feedback you can get is a sale, and one of my major accounts responded to my presentation by buying 20 percent more advertising than they did last year, and accepting several of our strong recommendations."

"This Magic Moment"

These are not people who loved speaking when they started. They are people just like you who wanted help, but weren't sure what the results would be.

Clint, representative for a state education association who was highly skeptical about taking the class: "Although I've been comfortable with other audiences, when working with teachers I've been so nervous I was close to being paralyzed. When I took your course I thought, 'I'm not going to remember all this three or four months down the road.' But here I was months after the course, training these teachers and using what I learned from you. I paused and focused. I remembered why they needed to know this information. It was wonderful. You don't realize how much you learn in a class like that until you go out and apply it."

Andy, corporate communications: "I was pretty amazed; the presentation actually was kind of fun, and you know it's never been one of my favorite things."

∙ ∙

"I felt great because I got my message across and said what I wanted to say."

∙ ∙

Harrie, attorney: "As you know, I had never intended to use notes, but I had planned to memorize it so there wouldn't be any chance of flubbing. But I'm glad I let you convince me that if we organized it in the most meaningful way, and I got to the heart of what the occasion and the person meant to me, that I could do it without the notes. I had thought I'd be really nervous in front of all those VIPs, but I focused on what the person I was honoring meant to me, and on what I wanted to say, (rather than on myself), and was aware of what I was doing and saying the whole time. I felt great because I got my message across and said what I wanted to say. I couldn't have asked for anything better."

Cheryl, contracts administration and material management: "I've used your picture-drawing suggestion (for notes) when preparing a 15-minute talk on a subject I'm not very familiar with. It works! Spending the time drawing helps visualize and really makes it easier to speak without notes. I was the only one in the group to do the presentation without notes and was praised for my spontaneity!"

Gary, comptroller: "I had a lot of fun with the first presentation I've given since taking your class. What we did in class helped me take a lot of complex data and boil it down to the essence of what the group needed and wanted to know, instead of drowning them in information."

. . . .

"This will stay with me throughout my career."

. . . .

Lisa, market research manager: "On the day before, I reviewed some of the key points I learned from your class. On the day of the presentation I was a bit shaky, but quickly recalled that you said I didn't have to be nervous. I started my talk by saying something personal. After that, I was just myself and for the next two hours was calm, in control, enthusiastic and had fun. It's the first time in my career I can honestly say I was not nervous during a presentation. This will stay with me throughout my career."

Dave, director of compensation and organization development, when asked to give a presentation to the company's president: "Before your class, I would have been scared spitless. Instead, I was excited that I was going to get to do it."

. . . .

"I'm looking forward to presenting . . . rather than having nightmares."

. . . .

Hal, corporate quality assurance manager: "I gave a speech at a recent symposium to 50-plus total strangers! If this were in my previous life, I wouldn't even have dreamed of it. But, of course, all I really thought about was how to transfer my enthusiasm on the subject to the audience. I stood still pretty well, smiled a few times, and even cracked two unprepared jokes people chuckled at! I conducted the Q & A session and handled 10-12 questions. All this the day after a 12-day European trip and no rehearsal. I need to prepare and practice some more, but the key fact is, I am looking forward to presenting and to the discussion, rather than having nightmares."

Lynda, strategic planning advisor: "It was so much fun; I'm still coming off a high. Sometimes I pinch myself, and ask myself, 'Was that really me?' Your class and that speech gave me so much self-confidence because I found I can express myself to others, to really share what I'm thinking with other people. I felt connected to the audience, and I felt more whole because I could actually be myself. The worst part was sitting in the front row waiting for my turn. And now I know I'll never let myself feel that way again. You don't have to go through that anxiety. That's exciting."

Steve, CEO and president: "You'll be glad to know I resisted the temptation to write out my talk and read it to the group while at the same time fumbling around with overhead slides. Instead, I remembered the principles from your seminar. I made sure I was well-prepared and comfortable with my material and wrote down only three short bullet points I wanted to emphasize. I stayed focused on my audience and tried to make eye contact with everyone in the room at some point during my talk. I found myself, within a few minutes, talking to my audience instead of just talking at them. The real benefit of not reading my material or relying on notes was the freedom I had to move back and forth from the lectern to the overhead projector without losing my place or getting disorganized. The result was 40 minutes in front of a large group without the old feelings of terror and anxiety."

Marlene, national sales manager: "On the last day of our three-day class, I felt great about what we'd heard and done in class, but I was really concerned about whether or not I'd be able to remember and use it all.

· ·

"You can practice all those principles even when you're not giving a speech."

· ·

That was three months ago. I no longer wonder. I think about it and use it almost every day. You were right— you can practice all those principles even when you're not giving a speech. It's all so logical and sensible that it's easy to remember and use. I love it."

"Follow the Yellow Brick Road"

At the end of the Yellow Brick Road, Dorothy, the Tin Man, the Cowardly Lion and the Scarecrow realized that the power to make dreams reality comes from within.

Tapping into that power is what this book has been about. By now I hope you have come to realize that effective, memorable and painless public speaking is a skill all of us can master.

Remember—public speaking:

- Is not about you.
  Every day, take time to notice how little
  other people pay attention to the little
  things that once seemed so significant
  to us.

- Is not just about providing information.
  If you focus only on the information you
  have to share, you'll eventually wind
  up focused on yourself.

- Is primarily about connecting with your
  audience.

Need more reminders? Take a look at these on the following page:

MANAGING YOUR LIFE

"ANYTHING [I] CAN DO, I CAN DO BETTER"

15

"Feelin' Groovy"

"And All That Jazz"

At the beginning of this book, I mentioned someone in my first class improved her bowling average 20 points—just from taking the class! What is that all about?

Well, this is a book about public speaking. But is that all it's about?

No, indeed. Getting over yourself when giving a speech is just the beginning. The speech goes better when you get out of the way, and so does everything else.

Perhaps you, too, have started using these principles for something other than speaking.

Speaking in public is, well, it's so public; it's hard to get over feeling as though all eyes are on us. Sadly, we then anticipate all the things that might go wrong.

It's not so different in daily life: whenever we anticipate possible calamities, or feel like the center of attention, we get self-conscious (conscious of ourselves).

So, if you're bowling, you might focus on being the center of attention, on how your clothing, bowling form or score look to the people on your team or to others in the bowling alley.

My student who improved her bowling average 20 points stopped focusing on these superficial things and began focusing on why she was there: to knock down pins (the main issue, after all).

What are some of your uncomfortable moments, when you don't feel as in control of yourself as you'd like? Times when you'd like to be invisible?

Meeting new people? Networking? Going to the gym? Interviewing for a job? Reading at church?

If you use the speaking principles in this book, you'll find you can learn to be invisible everywhere. It's only feeling we've got something to lose that keeps us from focusing on the main issue.

"Freedom's Just Another Word For Nothin' Left To Lose"

Let's say you're going to meet your girlfriend's parents for the first time. Naturally you want to make a good impression, and yet it's so important, you find it hard not to concentrate on your inadequacies,—things that haven't gone well in the past.

Just as in a speech, the secret is to start focusing on what you want to accomplish and how you can set your audience (in this case, her parents) at ease.

The less you focus on yourself and the more you focus on being gracious, and on making her parents comfortable, the easier it is to make a good impression.

Not focusing on yourself sets you free to listen to their stories, notice if you're dribbling your soup, and avoid saying things better left unsaid.

How to be invisible at the gym

I have a friend who won't go to the gym if she thinks anyone else will be there: she doesn't want anyone to see her in her workout clothes. She's probably a size 4, but she's sure everyone will be looking at her (unnoticeable to anyone else) saddle bags.

Recently I noticed a woman at the gym who definitely was not invisible—she wore a hooded sweatshirt with the hood pulled well over her head, covering most of her face. She probably didn't want anyone to notice her, but she created just the opposite effect.

If you want to be invisible at the gym, you're probably better off not wearing sequinned spandex, but a hooded sweatshirt doesn't work, either.

Another woman wearing serious work out attire made an elaborate ritual of donning special gloves, wrist guards and weight belt before approaching to pick up one lb. weights for her session.

The essence of invisibility is looking the way people expect you to look in those circumstances. Middle of the road attire and demeanor doesn't attract unwanted attention.

And it's also useful to be clear where people are focused when they are at the gym—it's the same place they're focused when you're giving a presentation—on themselves. (What do you think all those mirrors are there for?)

These are the five reasons people look at you at the gym, and the first four are the most likely: 1. They're staring into space in your direction and don't even see you. 2. They're really looking in the mirror at themselves. 3. They're checking out the exercise you're doing to see if it's something they ought to add to their workout. 4. They're wondering when you'll be through with that machine. And a *very* distant 5. They're actually interested in you. In which case, make the most of it.

If people notice you at the gym, they're still thinking of themselves—if they look better or worse than you, or if they could get a date with you. It's all about them.

"I Wish That I Knew What I Know Now When I Was Younger"

Oh, how we wish we could make life easier at school for our kids, easier than it was for us. The whole boy/girl thing, the self-consciousness, and the anxiety of giving oral reports. Most parents graphically remember the pain of speaking in front of the class.

We can help our children, with the same principles we're using for ourselves: "It's not about you." What a boost to help them do better in their studies and get a good foundation for getting into a better university, college, or first job.

It's never easy being a kid. And the faster pace of life, the speeded up social expectations, and greater competition for higher education slots continues to make it more difficult.

It would be great to have a magic pill to help kids get over themselves, 'cause this is major "it's all about me" time: learning the ground rules of life, looking for a personal identity, needing to be liked.

In lieu of a magic pill, here are some ways to help your kids get better grades, be more attractive to friends and give better presentations—even better speeches when running for office.

- We're all in the same boat. People who look like they know what they're doing are usually just good at faking it. Don't let them intimidate you.

- In front of the class, focus on your message. Will what you're telling them help them pass a test, decide whether or not to read a particular book, or understand something the class needs to know?

- Choose not to be nervous by focusing on outcomes and your own interest rather than the effect you're having on the group.

- And when you don't know what to do or say, pause and breathe, something will come to you, or you'll continue to pause and breathe and just look incredibly poised.

- Focus on looking for common interests rather than focusing on yourself and you're bound to get better results.

- And focus is the key when looking for better grades: focus on what goes on in class, and in test taking, focus on one question at a time rather than how the outcome of the test can affect your life.

"I Feel Pretty and Witty and Wise"

Why is it so hard to say good things about ourselves? It not only can be done, it can be done appropriately so no one else feels uncomfortable. It can be done and it should be done.

In our seminars, everyone is asked to say (a minimum of) two good things about their own videotaped speeches before they can say anything else about it. It is almost painful for most people to do this. There's a lot of squirming followed finally by "I can't think of anything good."

Yet, invariably, everyone else in the room can think of more than two good things to say. Of course, they have the same trouble finding good things about their own presentations.

The truth is, in order to get better, it's important to recognize what you're already doing well, so you can concentrate on things that need fine tuning.

And it's important for your children, too: Are you helping them recognize what they are doing well and what they should concentrate on improving?

On the one hand, we may withhold praise so as not to spoil. On the other, we may, with the best intentions, indiscriminately praise children for everything. This praising in an attempt to create "self-esteem" may have the opposite effect: it may also cause them to be petulant when others don't praise them for everything, or to perform only for a reward of some kind.

Another possible outcome: eventually, they may realize everything they do can't be that great and therefore not only doubt the sincerity of the praise, but to question everything else the praiser says to them.

Being able to objectively assess that which we do well and that which we need to work on is priceless for children and adults alike. Try it at least once a day.

Enough About Me. What Do YOU Think About Me?

There is a certain group of people (you know who you are) who have a most difficult time asking for directions.

And another group who are fine asking for directions but less comfortable going to a party without having the right thing to wear, or arriving late, or not knowing anyone. Or how about being too embarrassed to ask which fork to use, or what the person's name is—again.

Getting over yourself can take many forms; sometimes it's worrying what other people think of you and at other times it's worrying about living up to your own image of yourself.

One woman in one of our seminars made it quite clear that her problem speaking to an audience had nothing to do with what the audience thought about her, she couldn't bear disappointing herself. If she did or said something that wasn't as planned it upset her. Forget the audience—how could *she* live with her "imperfection?"

There's a bit of that in not asking for directions: "I should be able to figure this out myself." (One hopes the asker isn't concerned about what a stranger thinks about your asking for directions.)

Or being unwilling to ask someone to repeat their name (that you've forgotten) may feel like you're letting yourself down or that you'll look bad to the other person.

Showing up in the wrong outfit for that occasion can cause a momentary discomfort, or ruin the whole evening (depending on your attitude).

A friend of a friend attended a Bastille Day party (in the United States) wearing what he thought to be a bril-liant costume (no ordinary kingly costume for him). He came as a piece of cake. And wasn't he surprised when he arrived to find it wasn't a costume party. He stayed and had a marvelous time. What choice would you have made? (Okay, you prob-ably wouldn't have gone as a piece of cake in the first place.)

The solution in all these situations is still the same: you have a choice as to how to respond and how to feel. If your focus is on the outcome and not on your own or other's expectations, the choice you make will be the right one.

The Door Swings Both Ways or "Everybody's Looking for Something"

Job interviews and performance appraisals (whether you're on the giving or receiving end) also fall into the category of "it's not about me."

DILBERT Scott Adams

DILBERT reprinted by permission of United Features Syndicate, Inc.

Of course, you can come up with reasons why it *is* about you, but it's much more effective to come up with reasons why it isn't. For instance:

- A job interview goes two ways; you're both looking for a good fit. You don't want to be there if it's not the right place for you. You're looking for a way to contribute.

- The interviewer has more to lose than you do. If they hire the wrong person it's expensive and makes them look bad.

- When you look at it as a search, you stand taller and speak more confidently. You'll be looking to solve a problem rather than trying to impress the interviewer.

- A performance appraisal (also a two-way street) is a time for both people to look for ways to make their department and company more productive and profitable.

It's more effective to focus on reasons such as these, because we proceed freely when we feel confident, and choke when we're less sure.

Applying for a job when you don't need it engenders a whole different confidence level than applying for a job when you've been out of work a couple of months. So stay focused on why it's not about you.

A young man I met on an airplane as he travelled to his first job interview said, "That sounds great! I'm going to use those ideas. It's sure not what I've been taught about interviewing. Everything I've learned has really made me focus on being sure I give all the right answers."

"How Great Thou Art," or "Crying In The Chapel"

A number of people have reported that what they learned about speaking in one of our seminars has helped them be more comfortable and effective as lay readers in church.

It ought to be easy to know it's not about you in church because you didn't write the words and the message is about healing and reconciliation. But when we lose sight of that, it's right back to worrying about how we look and sound and what people will think.

There's the added pressure that we may not sound spiritual enough or that the congregation may be noting that we're not really pure enough for the job.

The breakthrough in effectiveness and comfort level comes at the point of letting go of the "noise" and self doubts, and focusing on the meaning of the message.

"Welcome To My World"

Any time we're in a new situation there's the possibility of feeling uncomfortable: at a party, meeting new in-laws, networking, etc. It's always more fun if you're comfortable. And getting over yourself makes it possible. It's about giving yourself permission.

When you go to a function and you're the designated greeter, most people automatically accept that as permission to walk up to people they don't know and make sure that person feels welcome and gets appropriate directions as to what to do next. And they'll do it with or without a badge.

When you give the same attention to making sure people feel welcome, comfortable, at ease in any situation you'll get the same result. You'll be perceived as gracious, credible and friendly and you'll also feel focused and at ease.

"I Want To Talk About Me"

Ralph Waldo Emerson said, "You set your own price." So, we decide whether people notice us or not.

There are times we want to be noticed and times we don't. When we do something incredibly intelligent, when we look great, when we make a hole-in-one, we love the attention.

When we spill coffee, have a bad hair day, make a less than brilliant suggestion it's a whole different story.

We direct others to pay attention to us when we're feeling awkward. We do it by apologizing inappropriately or drawing their attention to our perceived inadequacies in some way—getting the attention we don't really want.

When we feel on top, we walk, talk, and participate with more energy, focus and confidence. We naturally get noticed because those qualities attract attention.

People want to be a part of this winning act. So, unintentionally, we've directed them to pay attention to us. But it's okay, 'cause we're feelin' good.

"Time Is On My Side, Yes It Is"

Because none of us has enough time to get everything done, here's how "getting over yourself" can add more time to your day.

If you want more time in your life, do one thing at a time. Granted, there are times multitasking works for people, but you have to know where it absolutely won't work.

For instance, you've got a big 'to do' list facing you and you're thinking about that as you talk to one of your managers. Maybe you're delegating a project, or giving a compliment, but in either case being "elsewhere" wastes time and loses a chance to build your team. It will come back to bite you and that will require more of your time.

To get the most out of the communication, focus: Focus on what you're saying and focus on the other person's reaction. Be present. Give this your full attention. That person will take it more seriously, is more likely to follow through (or have a glow of feeling appreciated if it was a compliment), and you're less likely to have to revisit or repair the situation.

Paying attention to one thing at a time when you're dealing with people makes them feel important, makes it more likely they, too, will pay attention, and makes it more likely you'll say what you wanted to say.

5 + 2 = 60

Being present—being in the moment—can not only buy you time, but devotion as well, including in your family.

People often talk about "quality time" but find it hard to honor it. A simple formula might be the solution: Five minutes plus two people = 60 minutes. Giving 5 minutes of focused attention to someone—significant other, child, coworker—can deliver the benefits of 60 minutes. Now there's a time saver that can definitely be a relationship saver.

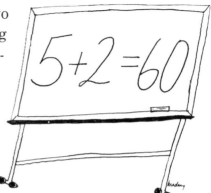

"Oh, Say Can You See?"

What do you do if you're singing the National Anthem at a televised basketball game in front of a large audience and you go blank? There it was on the news the other night: a young woman lost the words, lost the notes, and, in short, lost it. The basketball coach moved up next to her and coached her through her distressing moment.

Her particular embarrassing moment won't be one that most of us will have to endure, but what of our own personal forgettable moments?

Those are the perfect moments to remember "it's not about me." In the case of losing the song in front of a huge audience, naturally your first thought would be that it IS about me. But that won't lead you to a solution. And there won't always be someone who feels equal responsibility for the occasion (such as the coach) who will step up and help you out.

If you thought, "this is not about me," you might ask the audience to help you out by singing along, because you're pretty sure that's one song most of your audience knows. And they'd rather help you out than watch you suffer.

Or, you might focus on the words and the notes and get back on track.

In any case, you'd come up with a solution that would set the audience at ease and make you feel good about yourself.

"What's It All About, Alfie?"

What it boils down to is, anything I can do, I can do better—if I get out of my own way.

Without taking a single lesson, you can improve your golf, tennis, dancing, singing, test taking, interviewing—by getting out of the way.

Remembering Nike's slogan, "You're either in the zone or you're in the way," points us in the right direction. You've probably been in the zone in some aspect of your life; and as you look back you can see you were in the zone because you weren't getting in the way by focusing on technique or personalities.

Getting over yourself blesses you and everyone around you. Practice getting out of the way in any area of your life, and you'll automatically begin to connect the dots in other areas as well. Try it. You'll love the results!

BUMPER STICKER
PHILOSOPHY of SPEAKING

There is no such thing as a boring subject—only bored speakers

Refuse to be BORED

Most audiences are human

Be HUMAN

You can be any kind of speaker you choose to be

Choose to be GOOD

BASIC BARB - INDEX

Anxiety
  Banishing it, 17-18

Appearance
  What we notice, 11-12
  What to wear, 12-14

Approachability
  Benefits of, 78-79

Aristotle
  On getting reactions, 166

Attitude
  To avoid suffering, 23-24
  On perfection, 25-26

Audiences
  Coping with hostility, 90-95
  How to think like one, 59-60
  What they want, 61-64

Berra, Yogi
  On crossroads, 19
  When it's over, 74

Body
  Of speech, 135-138

Boredom
  How it happens, 63
  Refusing to be, 159, 187
  Using visual aids, 162

Bowling,
  Improving your game, Author's
  Notes and 186

Brain lock
  How to get past it, 40-42

Breathing
  Is good, 80-81
  For relaxation, 81
  To calm fear, 19, 80-81

Bridges
  Between opening/thesis, 145-148
  Connecting to the audience, 132
  In impromptu talks, 153-154
  In organizing a speech, 148
  Mario Cuomo as an example, 146

Buchwald, Art
  Information Highway, 156

Bush, Barbara
  On tough crowds, 155

Carlsson, Ingvar
  Speaking to audience concerns, 146

Choice
  For empowerment, 19
  Game plans, 56

Choke chains
  Imaginary, 21-22

Church
  Reading in, 198

Churchill, Winston
  Make it short, 138

Clinton, Bill
  Speaking style, 100-101

Clothes
  Appropriateness, 12
  Inappropriateness, 193
  New ones, 13

Closing
  Organization, 132
  Socko finish, 138-140
  Wrapping up, 74-75

Complimenting
  Yourself, 194

Confidence
  Building it, 57-59, 86
  What it does, 85, 156

Connecting
  With your audience, 66-67
  Being in the moment, 200

Control
  Losing it, 57
  Maintaining it, 58-59

Cooking Class
  Lesson to learn from, 8

Cuomo, Mario
  Example of using bridge, 146

Directions,
  Asking for, 192-3

Disaster
  How to overcome, 32-34

Discomfort
  Meeting parents, going to a
  party, 188-189

Driver, Jessica Somers
  On poise, 39

Einstein, Albert
  On relativity, 41

Embarrassment
  Overcoming, 201

Eye contact
  Calming, 109
  Caring, 108
  Seeing, 110
  Keeping focus, 110

Fear
  How to cope, 16
  Of hostile audiences, 89
  You're not alone, 15

Feeling good
  About speaking, 20-21
  About yourself, 194

Fight or flight syndrome, 80

Focus
  Losing it, 35-36, 46-47, 50
  How to regain, 40, 46-47, 51-52
  To allay fear, 19, 21, 75
  Using the PREP formula, 152-153

Forbes, Steve
  Vivid imagery, 158

Ford, Henry
  On ideas, 47

Gestures
  As visual aids, 102-105
  Bill Clinton, 100
  How they help keep focus, 104
  Richard Nixon, 103-104
  What to avoid, 100-105

Glaser, Elizabeth
  At the Democratic Convention, 139

Goofs, 31-32

Gramm, Phil
Homespun analogies, 158

Hands
Effective use, 104-105
What to do with, 101-103

Horowitz, Vladimir
Moment most important, 50

Hostility
Defusing with humor, 92
In audience, 90-96

Humor
Defusing hostility, 92
Jokes, 144
When to use, 144-145

Impromptu speeches
Being ready, 152
PBFL, 154
Practice, 159
Question and answer sessions, 154

Inflection
Mixed signals, 112
Tone of voice, 113-114

Introductions
Do your homework, 168
Keeping focused, 167-168

Invisibility
Achieving, 9-11, 39, 74
At the gym, 191-192

Kennedy, John F.
Using humor to diffuse issues, 92

Kids
Helping them grow, 190-192
Praising, 192

Kuehl, Sheila
On being friendly, 90

Lecterns
Letting go, 115-117
Note holder, 117
Proper use, 117-118

Lennon, John
Life is . . . , 32

Listening
Benefit: have more time, 200
Benefit: get more love, 200-201
How to do it better, 48-50
What it is, 46-47
Why it's so important, 49, 67

Mazlow, Abraham
Theory of learning, 178

Midori
Poise personified, 37

Mistakes
Dealing with, 31-38

National Anthem
Forgetting, 199

Ned's Rules
Elements of technical
presentations, 172
Organizing, 170
Visuals, 171

Nervousness
  How to overcome, 17-21
  Irrational behavior, 19

Nixon, Richard
  Bad gestures, 103-104, 110
  Perfection, 28

Notes
  As visuals, 122
  Avoiding them, 118-120
  Looking at, 118, 122
  Using pictures as, 120-122

Openings
  And the bridge, 153-154
  Connecting, 145-146
  Examples, 142-143

Organization
  Getting started, 131-136
  Options, 149
  PREP formula, 152-153

Outlines
  The principle of, 149-150

Pacing
  Drawbacks, 99-100

Panic
  Avoiding, 17-19
  Disastrous, 43

Parts of a speech, 131-132

Pauses
  Effective use of, 42-43, 93, 154
  Relativity, 41-42
  What they do, 38, 122
  What to avoid, 41

PBFL, 154

Perfection
  Hazards of trying, 26-28
  Vs. being human, 30

Personal
  Don't take it that way, 21, 39,
  83, 90-96, 185

Persuasion
  Win them over, 155-157

Poise
  Defined, 36
  How to get it, 38-40
  Roots of, 39

Posture
  Looking confident, 107-108
  Walk tall, 106

Powell, Colin
  On dreams, 139
  On time limits, 127
  Pause and effect, 43

PREP, 152-153

Presentations
  Parts of, 131-132

Rabin, Yitzhak
  Connecting to the audience, 66

Reagan, Ronald
  Great Communicator, 157
  Humor, hope, 92
  Rhythm, 69

Rhythm
Capitalizing on, 68-69
Your audience's, 67-68
Your own, 67-68

Rooney, Andy
Explaining Federal Deficit, 73

Rudeness,
Dealing with, 94-96

Selling
Basis of, 64-66

Silence
Effective use of, 41-42
When it's bad, 43

Sleep
Losing, 81-82
Putting an audience to, 83

Stone, Edward J.
Ned's Rules, 170-172

Stringer, Vivian,
On dressing well, 12

Techies
Are people too, 69

Technical presentations
Rules that apply, 69-72

Thesis statements
And the PREP formula, 152-153
What they are, 134-138, 142

Time limits
How to cope, 127-131

Transitions
Taking the audience through a
change, 150-152

Verbal fillers
Stop using, 105-108

Voice
Inflection, 112-114

Visuals
A song, 169
Gestures as, 102, 104
Handouts, 70, 166
Ned's Rules, 170-172
Notes as, 165
Pitfalls, 7, 166, 173
When to use, 74, 161-163,
165-166, 174

Walking
Onto stage, 107

Yeltsin, Boris
Selling an idea, 139

Young, Edward D. III
In the act of selling, 139
On visuals, 164
Thesis statement and
structure, 135-137

Zone
Being in the, 202

Cartoons

Sally Forth .... p. 3, 18, 84
Blondie .... p. 5, 58
Peanuts .... p. 8, 43, 56
Berry's World .... p. 13
Ballard Street .... p. 16
Merle .... p. 17, 37
Hagar the Horrible .... p. 19
Mister Boffo .... p. 46
Kudzu .... p. 48
Calvin and Hobbes .... p. 49, 72, 111
Baby Blues .... p. 62
Dilbert .... p. 70, 128, 164, 167, 197
For Better or for Worse .... p. 105
Bent Offerings .... p. 108, 163
Grin and Bear It .... p. 112
Francie .... p. 119
Crock .... p. 144
Real Live Adventures .... p. 153
Beetle Baily .... p. 162, 168

Order Form

🖎   Fax orders Toll Free: (888) 253-2330

☎   Telephone orders Toll Free: (888) 800-2001 Have your credit card ready.

💻   On-line orders: Orders@GettingOverYourself.com

✉   Postal orders: Bouldin Hill Press,
         PO Box 60521, Pasadena, CA 91116-6521
         Tel: (888) 800-2001 (626) 792-8075

Please send the following items:

___ *Getting Over Yourself: A Guide to Painless Public Speaking and More* (book) $19.95

___ Companion video (50 minutes: highlights and excerpts from classes) $99

___ CD ($19.95) or Audiotape ($17.95) of *Getting Over Yourself* read by author

Pocket-size books $9.95 each

___ *Pocket Guide for Presenters* 110 pages

___ *60 Ways to Spark Your Speaking: Just in Time Answers to Frequently Asked Questions* 160 pages

___ *Love to Talk, Hate to Speak? How to Gain Confidence in Front of Any Audience* 126 pages

___ Speech on ( ) CD or ( ) Audiotape: *From Bored Room to Board Room* $10.95

___ Speech on ( ) CD or ( ) Audiotape: *Stand Up and Stand Out* $10.95

☐   Please add me to your FREE *"FOCUS on Business Speaking"* e-newsletter list.

Company name: _____

Name: _____

Address: _____

City: _____ State:_____ Zip:_____-_____

Telephone: ( )_____ Ext._____ E-mail: _____

Sales tax:
Please add 7.75% for books shipped to California addresses.

Shipping:
$3.50 for the first book or video and $2.00 for each additional unit.

Payment:
☐   Check
☐   Credit card: ☐VISA ☐MasterCard ☐American Express

Name on card: _____

Card number: _____ Exp. date: _____/_____

Call *toll free* and order now
Visit our website: www.GettingOverYourself.com

Order Form

✂   Fax orders Toll Free: (888) 253-2330

☎   Telephone orders Toll Free: (888) 800-2001 Have your credit card ready.

💻   On-line orders: Orders@GettingOverYourself.com

✉   Postal orders: Bouldin Hill Press,
     PO Box 60521, Pasadena, CA 91116-6521
     Tel: (888) 800-2001 (626) 792-8075

Please send the following items:

___ *Getting Over Yourself: A Guide to Painless Public Speaking and More* (book) $19.95

___ Companion video (50 minutes: highlights and excerpts from classes) $99

___ CD ($19.95) or Audiotape ($17.95) of *Getting Over Yourself* read by author

Pocket-size books $9.95 each

___ *Pocket Guide for Presenters* 110 pages

___ *60 Ways to Spark Your Speaking: Just in Time Answers to Frequently Asked Questions* 160 pages

___ *Love to Talk, Hate to Speak? How to Gain Confidence in Front of Any Audience* 126 pages

___ Speech on ( ) CD or ( ) Audiotape: *From Bored Room to Board Room* $10.95

___ Speech on ( ) CD or ( ) Audiotape: *Stand Up and Stand Out* $10.95

☐   Please add me to your FREE *"FOCUS on Business Speaking"* e-newsletter list.

Company name: _____

Name: _____

Address: _____

City: _____ State:_____ Zip:_____-_____

Telephone: (   )_____ Ext._____ E-mail: _____

Sales tax:
Please add 7.75% for books shipped to California addresses.

Shipping:
$3.50 for the first book or video and $2.00 for each additional unit.

Payment:
☐   Check
☐   Credit card: ☐VISA ☐MasterCard ☐American Express

Name on card: _____

Card number: _____Exp. date: _____/_____

Call *toll free* and order now
Visit our website: www.GettingOverYourself.com